150 BEST
TOASTER OVEN
RECIPES

D1616573

LINDA STEPHEN

Robert
ROSE

To Bill Vronsky

————————•————————

150 Best Toaster Oven Recipes
Text copyright © 2018 Linda Stephen
Photographs copyright © 2018 Robert Rose Inc.
Cover and text design copyright © 2018 Robert Rose Inc.

Some of the content of this book was previously published in *125 Best Toaster Oven Recipes*, published in 2004 by Robert Rose Inc.

No part of this publication may be reproduced, stored in a retrieval system or transmitted, in any form or by any means, without the prior written consent of the publisher or a licence from The Canadian Copyright Licensing Agency (Access Copyright). For an Access Copyright Licence, visit www.accesscopyright.ca or call toll-free to 1-800-893-5777.

For complete cataloguing information, see page 208.

Disclaimer
The recipes in this book have been carefully tested by our kitchen and our tasters. To the best of our knowledge, they are safe and nutritious for ordinary use and users. For those people with food or other allergies, or who have special food requirements or health issues, please read the suggested contents of each recipe carefully and determine whether or not they may create a problem for you. All recipes are used at the risk of the consumer. Consumers should always consult their toaster oven manufacturer's manual for recommended procedures and cooking times.

We cannot be responsible for any hazards, loss or damage that may occur as a result of any recipe use.

For those with special needs, allergies, requirements or health problems, in the event of any doubt, please contact your medical advisor prior to the use of any recipe.

Editor: Shelley Tanaka
Proofreader: Kelly Jones
Indexer: Gillian Watts
Design & Production: PageWave Graphics Inc.

Photo Insert Pages 6, 8–10, 12, 14–16:
Photography: Mark T. Shapiro
Food Styling: Kate Bush
Prop Styling: Charlene Erricson
Photo Insert Pages 1–5, 7, 11, 13:
Photography: Tango Photography
Food Styling: Éric Régimbald
Prop Styling: Véronique Gagnon-Lalanne

Cover image: Deli Tuna Melts (page 13)

The publisher gratefully acknowledges the financial support of our publishing program by the Government of Canada through the Canada Book Fund.

Canada

Published by Robert Rose Inc.
120 Eglinton Avenue East, Suite 800, Toronto, Ontario, Canada M4P 1E2
Tel: (416) 322-6552; Fax: (416) 322-6936

Printed in Canada

1 2 3 4 5 6 7 8 9 MI 26 25 24 23 22 21 20 19 18

FSC® MIX Paper from responsible sources FSC® C103567

Contents

Acknowledgments

MANY THANKS to the same group of friends and professionals who brought together my previous cookbook:

- Beverly MacArtney Melnick of Cuisinart Canada.
- Bob Dees, Kelly Glover and the team at Robert Rose Inc.; Alicia McCarthy and Kevin Cockburn at PageWave Graphics; Pierre Lafreniere, Éric Régimbald and Véronique Gagnon-Lalanne at Tango Photography; Mark Shapiro, Kate Bush and Charlene Ericcson; Jennifer MacKenzie.
- Doris Stephen, my mother, friend and supporter.
- Rhonda and Fred Caplan, Josée Ménard, the Klein household, the Stephen households, the Livingston household, and my neighbors, who endured multiple testings and tastings.
- Bonnie Stern, Maureen Lollar, Barb Holland, Gord Ley and Glen Gardner, for their help and inspiration.
- Kim Pedersen, for her encouragement and technical assistance.
- Shelley Tanaka, for pushing and encouraging me.

Introduction

I SAW MY FIRST TOASTER OVEN twenty years ago, when I was staying with a friend who used it to toast bread and bagels. But I didn't get one of my own until I wrote *The Best Convection Oven Cookbook*, which included a chapter of convection toaster oven recipes. That's when I first started to actually cook in the toaster oven, and right away I was hooked.

Over the many years that I have been cooking, teaching and catering, I have become used to cooking meals for anywhere from six to two hundred people. So it was second nature for me to turn on the big kitchen oven when I was at home, even when I was cooking for just a few people.

Then I realized that this convenient countertop item was really just a tiny oven, and that it really could cook. I could make entire meals for three or four in it. I could bake cakes, pies and bread in it. I could roast and broil in it. And I could even use it for reheating and toasting bread and bagels! Now the toaster oven is a permanent appliance in my kitchen.

Not only convenient for students, singles, young couples, empty-nesters and retirees, the toaster oven is also ideal for families. Kids can easily learn to make themselves nachos, mini pizzas and French toast. It's perfect for whipping up a Spaghetti Pie (page 118) for a weekday meal, or Beef Tenderloin (page 96) and Baked Alaska (page 200) for a special-occasion dinner for two.

And at a time when we are all faced with soaring energy costs and even blackouts, consumers are becoming more aware of how much energy large appliances use. Why turn on the big oven when the toaster oven will do the same task?

As a cautious consumer and veteran cook, it takes me a long time to change my habits and equipment. But I have quickly become a cheerleader and advocate of the toaster oven, and I now use it almost daily.

And my friend? She now has a stepped-up model of a toaster oven that she uses more often than she uses her standard oven.

About Toaster Ovens

THE TOASTER OVEN has come a long way from being a glorified toaster that simply toasts bagels and open-face cheese sandwiches to an appliance that cooks everything from a roast chicken to muffins and casseroles — dishes that have traditionally been prepared only in a standard-sized oven. Many toaster ovens now include features such as touch-pad controls, defrost and reheat options, convection option, timers, clocks, easy-clean interiors, cool touch exteriors and more. There are even new microwave/toaster ovens and models that combine a toaster oven with a rotisserie and griddle.

Much smaller than a standard oven, this versatile appliance is convenient, space-saving and energy-efficient, and it is becoming a permanent item in many kitchens. Always a popular appliance for students, toaster ovens are now used by single professionals, young couples, empty-nesters, occasional cooks and retirees. They are a boon for large families, too — easily operated by kids, and a handy second oven when you are entertaining and need extra oven space.

When you buy, think beyond toasting and reheating. Consider your needs and how you would likely use your oven. Most ovens will toast, bake and broil. Some have defrost, reheat and convection options. Choose a well-known brand to ensure a good warranty and available servicing, if required.

Many consumers make the mistake of selecting an oven that is too small. Then when they discover how versatile this oven is, they wish they had purchased a larger unit. It will often become their main or permanent oven.

Check the capacity (some can roast a 4-lb/2 kg chicken and accommodate a 13-by 9-inch/3.5 L baking dish), exterior (cool touch), surface (easy clean), accessories and the external dimensions (for your available space). Some consumers install a special shelving unit (check the manufacturer's manual to make sure there is adequate space between the oven and the back wall, and that the oven is not enclosed).

ADVANTAGES

- A toaster oven is more energy efficient than a full-sized oven (using about half as much energy as a standard oven). It is also the fraction of the price of a standard oven.
- Toaster ovens preheat very quickly. When I first used the toaster oven, I would turn it on before I started to do anything else (as instructed in many cookbooks), but the oven would reach the cooking temperature before I had even assembled my ingredients! Preheat just before you are ready to use the oven (many will preheat to 350°F/180°C in just three minutes).
- Since the toaster oven doesn't heat up the kitchen like a big stove or oven, it is especially good for use in the summer, at the cottage or in your recreational vehicle.
- The toaster oven is easy to clean. The slide-out trays and easy-clean interior walls make tidy-up simple, especially if you wipe up any spills as soon as they occur.

- A toaster oven is light and portable, and it takes up minimal counter space, making it ideal for galley kitchens, student digs, cottages or RVs (check your manufacturer's manual for instructions on placement).
- Many toaster ovens will defrost and reheat, but unlike a microwave, the toaster oven produces crisp and crusty results when desired.

OVEN FEATURES

The toaster oven comes with an oven pan (also called oven tray), a broiler rack (drip tray) and the oven rack (toaster rack). In some models, the oven rack has two positions and can also be inverted so that the food is closer to or farther from the heat source. The oven pan can double as a baking sheet for cookies, biscuits and free-form breads.

Most models have a removable crumb tray for easy cleaning.

OVEN SETTINGS

Most toaster ovens have three main functions:

Toast

The **Toast** function is for toasting breads of varying thickness, bagels and sandwiches. In most ovens, the lightness or darkness can be adjusted. Some ovens have a special setting for bagels and four slices of toast.

To toast, place the item directly on the oven rack, making sure that the crumb tray is in position. (Never wrap the oven rack or crumb tray with foil, as this can cause the oven to overheat.) Use this setting for toasting English muffins, crumpets and breads. Pizzas and pastries can also be crisped using this setting.

Bake

The **Bake** function can be used to cook roasts, stews, casseroles, squares, cookies, pizzas, breads, cakes and desserts. The bake temperature can be set as in a regular oven.

Before you start to bake, make sure your baking dish will fit in the oven. Some baked dishes require covering, either with a lid or foil. If you use foil, make sure it fits tightly and is at least 2 inches (5 cm) away from the heat source.

Preheat the oven until the indicator light goes on or the signal sounds.

For the best results when baking items such as cakes, squares and breads, turn the pan partway through baking. (This may not be required in all cases; you will soon find out whether this is necessary with your oven for even browning.)

In some ovens the rack for the bottom setting can be inverted so it is slightly farther from the bottom heat source. If this optional rack setting is available, use it for squares and cakes. Pies, muffins and breads bake well on the lower rack.

As in any oven, the interior temperature fluctuates. This fluctuation may affect items that are baked for a short time (e.g., cookies). The interior temperature is also lowered every time you open the oven door. Some ovens are also better insulated than others, and the temperature may vary in different parts of the oven.

Check foods with short cooking times frequently. You will soon find out how your oven cooks and can adjust cooking times accordingly.

Broil

The **Broil** function is used for appetizers, grilled meat, fish or poultry. You can also use the broil setting for melting cheese toppings, browning casseroles or crisping items such as chicken wings.

Food should be placed at least 1 inch (2.5 cm) from the heat source. As the heat comes only from above, items may need to be turned to cook the second side.

The best results are achieved when food items are of uniform thickness.

Preheat the broiler according to the manufacturer's instructions. Most manufacturers recommend leaving the oven door ajar when broiling, but check your manual. Do not wrap the broiler rack in foil as splattering can occur as well as overheating. Always place the broiler rack over the oven pan. Some manufacturers recommend adding about $\frac{1}{4}$ cup (50 mL) water to the oven pan to reduce sizzling and splattering. Under high heat, some oven pans may also temporarily buckle during cooking.

Convection Bake

This is a fairly recent feature in toaster ovens. In convection cooking, hot air is circulated throughout the oven by a fan, creating moist and juicy interiors and browned surfaces especially suitable for roasts. Originally found only in large commercial ovens, the convection feature has been adapted to the standard home oven and is now available in some toaster ovens. However, unlike larger ovens, there is only one convection feature in the toaster oven — convection bake. The convection function does not operate when you are broiling or toasting.

Most foods will convection bake up to 30 percent faster than in conventional cooking, provided that nothing blocks the circulating air, such as lids, foil or high-sided dishes. The heat comes from both the bottom and top elements, and the fan circulates the air, encouraging all-over browning. With the convection bake feature, it may not be necessary to turn pans halfway through the cooking time, but check occasionally to make sure the dish is browning evenly.

The general rule of convection cooking is to reduce the oven temperature by 25°F (13°C) or reduce the cooking time by 25 to 30 percent. More time is saved the longer an item cooks.

When using the convection setting, mark the temperature and timing on your recipe for future reference.

COOKWARE

Your cupboards may already contain the cookware you need for your toaster oven. If you are shopping for new items, know the interior dimensions of your oven. Department stores, supermarkets and kitchenware shops also stock a good selection of foil bakeware, which is convenient for baking, storing, freezing and reheating dishes.

In addition to the broiler rack and oven pan that come with the oven, all the recipes in this book can be made using the following items:

- a 6-cup muffin pan
- a standard 8- by 4-inch (1.5 L) loaf pan
- a 6-cup (1.5 L) baking dish or casserole with lid
- an 8-cup (2 L) baking dish or casserole with lid
- an 8-inch (2 L) square glass or metal baking dish
- a 9-inch (23 cm) pie plate
- deep 8-inch (20 cm) and 9-inch (23 cm) round cake pans
- four 4-oz (125 mL) ramekins
- parchment paper and foil

GENERAL TIPS

- Always read the manufacturer's manual before using your oven.
- Use dry pot holders (wet pot holders or oven mitts conduct heat and can cause steam burns).

- Keep the crumb tray clean. Do not operate the oven without the crumb tray in place.
- Unplug the oven when it is not in use.
- Select a space in your kitchen where the oven is easily accessible. Allow enough space to open the oven door and room to place items going in and out of the oven. Do not crowd items around the oven or store items on top of it.
- Although the oven pan cleans well, some recipes contain ingredients that may stick, such as sugary marinades or sauces. For ease of clean-up, parchment paper can be cut to fit the bottom of the oven pan. Do not let the edges of the paper extend over the sides of the pan.
- Toaster ovens are more efficient if the door is left closed. If possible, try to check food by viewing through the glass door.
- Place foods at least 1 to 2 inches (2.5 to 5 cm) away from the elements (check your manufacturer's manual).
- The recipes in this book can also be prepared in a standard oven, but check doneness toward the end of the cooking time.

MAKE AHEAD

Certain recipes can be partially prepared ahead of time, covered and refrigerated. For good finishing results, it is recommended that the dish stand for up to 30 minutes at room temperature (68° to 70°F/20° to 21°C) before final baking or reheating to take off some refrigerator chill. In addition, many dishes can be completely cooked ahead, frozen or refrigerated and then reheated. (Don't forget that your toaster oven can also be used to heat up foods.)

FOOD SAFETY

- Wash your hands for 20 seconds before starting to cook and after coughing, sneezing, using the restroom and touching pets.
- Keep work surfaces, cutting boards and counter surfaces clean. Sanitize them with a mild chlorine bleach solution (especially when working with meats, poultry and seafood). Mix 1 tsp (5 mL) bleach with 3 cups (750 mL) water and store the bleach solution in a well-labeled spray bottle.
- Use two cutting boards: one for raw meat, poultry and fish; one for cooked foods, fresh vegetables and fruits.
- Keep cold foods cold, below 40°F (4°C).
- Keep hot foods hot, above 140°F (60°C).
- Keep raw meat, poultry and seafood separate from one another, other foods and cooked foods. Use clean utensils and dishes when switching from raw to cooked foods.
- Defrost meat, poultry and fish completely under refrigeration and keep in the refrigerator until cooking.
- Marinate foods in the refrigerator. Boil any remaining marinade for 7 minutes or discard it. Do not reuse raw marinades.
- Use a spoon to baste raw foods, as it is difficult to clean brushes thoroughly.
- Use a food/meat thermometer to check the internal temperature of foods.
- Refrigerate leftovers as quickly as possible. Cooling to room temperature on the counter invites bacteria growth. Use leftovers quickly.

RECOMMENDED SAFE TEMPERATURE FOR DONENESS

Beef and Lamb	*rare to medium-rare*	140°F (60°C)
	medium	160°F (70°C)
	well done	170°F (75°C)
Pork	*medium*	160°F (70°C)
Ground Beef and Pork	*well done*	170°F (75°C)
Ham (ready to eat and fully cooked)		140°F (60°C)
Whole Chicken and Turkey (unstuffed)		180°F (82°C)
Turkey Breast		170°F (75°C)
Ground Chicken and Turkey		175°F (80°C)

ABOUT THE RECIPES

- The recipes in this book have been developed to make the most of the toaster oven. Although most recipes make two to five servings, the occasional one will serve six or more.
- The recipes in this book were tested in a toaster oven with a 0.5 cubic-foot capacity and an interior measuring $11\frac{1}{2}$ inches (30 cm) wide, 6 inches (15 cm) high and 10 inches (25 cm) deep.

- The following were used unless otherwise specified: regular table salt, freshly ground black pepper, salted butter, 2 percent milk and yogurt, homemade or canned stock (canned broth diluted according to package instructions).
- Always taste and adjust seasonings at the end of the cooking time.

The Basics

Lemon Garlic Salmon

Baking fish fillets in foil gives them a moist, tender texture. If you prefer, you can omit the spinach. Steamed rice is an ideal accompaniment either way. When making this, I often prepare an extra fillet to have cold with lunch the next day.

MAKES 2 SERVINGS

Variation

Maple Lemon Salmon
Before wrapping salmon, drizzle with 2 tsp (10 mL) maple syrup.

2 cups	baby spinach	500 mL
1	clove garlic, thinly sliced	1
2	skinless salmon fillets (each about 6 oz/175 g)	2
½ tsp	dried dillweed (optional)	2 mL
¼ tsp	salt	1 mL
2 tsp	olive oil	10 mL
4	lemon slices	4

1. Arrange spinach and garlic on two sheets of foil, dividing evenly. Top each with a salmon fillet. Sprinkle with dill, if using, and salt. Drizzle with olive oil and top each with 2 lemon slices. Fold in foil edges and ends to seal. Place packages seam side up on oven pan.

2. Bake in preheated 400°F (200°C) toaster oven for 18 to 20 minutes, or until fish is opaque and flakes easily when tested with a fork (peek in one package to check). Remove from oven and let stand for 2 minutes. Open packages and drain off juices.

Deli Tuna Melts

Everyone has their own favorite version of tuna melts. This is similar to the ones we prepared when I was teaching junior high. Years later, I still meet these students, who are now making them for their families. Serve with extra dill pickles and perhaps coleslaw.

MAKES 2 SERVINGS

Variation

Tuna Melts with Tomato
Top each prepared tuna melt with 2 tomato slices (depending on the size of the tomato) before sprinkling with remaining cheese.

2	large slices rye or other favorite bread	2
1	6-oz (170 g) can tuna, drained and flaked	1
1	green onion, chopped	1
¾ cup	grated Cheddar cheese, divided	175 mL
3 tbsp	mayonnaise or unflavored Greek yogurt, or more	45 mL
2 tbsp	chopped dill pickle	25 mL
2 tbsp	chopped celery	25 mL

1. Arrange bread slices on oven pan (lined with foil or parchment paper for easy cleanup). Toast lightly in preheated 400°F (200°C) toaster oven for 5 minutes.

2. Meanwhile, in a bowl, combine tuna, green onion, ½ cup (125 mL) cheese, mayonnaise, pickle and celery. Mix thoroughly, adding more mayonnaise to taste, if desired.

3. Spread tuna mixture evenly over partially toasted bread slices. Sprinkle with remaining ¼ cup (50 mL) cheese.

4. Bake in toaster oven for 8 minutes, or until cheese is melted and tuna melts are hot. Cut each in half.

Fish Tacos

So quick and easy to make, fish tacos are almost an any-meal solution, excellent for brunch, lunch or dinner any day of the week. Flour tortillas are the traditional wrap, but corn tortillas, crispy shells or even lettuce leaves can be used. Lately, some supermarkets have been stocking flour tortilla "bowls." With a variety of toppings, everyone can customize their own taco.

MAKES 2 TO 3 SERVINGS

1 lb	frozen fish fillets (such as tilapia or cod), defrosted (or fresh fish fillets)	500 g
2 tsp	olive oil	10 mL
1 tbsp	lime juice	15 mL
½ tsp	garlic salt	2 mL
½ tsp	chili powder	2 mL
½ tsp	dried oregano leaves	2 mL
½ tsp	smoked or sweet paprika	2 mL
¼ tsp	ground cumin	1 mL
¼ tsp	black pepper	1 mL
4 to 6	flour or corn tortillas (5 to 6 inches/ 12.5 to 15 cm)	4 to 6

Optional Toppings

Shredded cabbage or lettuce

Guacamole

Salsa (page 54 or 65)

Diced jalapeños

1. Arrange fillets in a single layer on parchment-lined oven pan. Brush fish with olive oil and drizzle with lime juice.
2. In a small bowl, combine garlic salt, chili powder, oregano, paprika, cumin and pepper. Sprinkle fillets with spice mixture just to taste. (Store any leftover mixture for the next time you make tacos.)
3. Bake in preheated 375°F (190°C) toaster oven for 8 to 10 minutes, or until fish flakes easily when tested with a fork. (Timing depends on thickness of fish.)
4. Wrap tortillas in foil and heat in the toaster oven for 5 minutes while preparing toppings.

Taco Seasoning

Taco seasoning, available in supermarkets and bulk stores, can replace the spice mixture.

Garlic Shrimp and Broccoli

Here's a fresh, flavorful and colorful dish to serve as a "fancy" appetizer or, with steamed rice, as the main course. Some shrimp still have the tail attached. Although they make for a nice presentation, you may wish to remove the tails prior to baking.

MAKES 2 TO 3 SERVINGS

Variation

Although the recipe calls for frozen uncooked shrimp, frozen cooked shrimp can be substituted. Stir cooked shrimp into broccoli halfway through baking time. Bake until hot throughout.

8 oz	frozen uncooked deveined peeled shrimp (about 12 to 14)	250 g
2 cups	broccoli florets (smallish pieces)	500 mL
2	cloves garlic, finely chopped	2
$\frac{1}{2}$ tsp	salt	2 mL
$\frac{1}{4}$ tsp	hot red pepper flakes (optional)	1 mL
1 tbsp	olive oil	15 mL
2 tbsp	chopped fresh parsley or dillweed, or $\frac{1}{2}$ tsp (2 mL) dried	25 mL
2 tbsp	lemon juice	25 mL

1. Arrange shrimp and broccoli in an 8-inch (2 L) baking dish or casserole. Sprinkle with garlic, salt and hot pepper flakes, if using. Drizzle with olive oil. Toss to combine ingredients.

2. Bake in preheated 400°F (200°C) toaster oven for 18 to 20 minutes, stirring once, until broccoli is tender and shrimp are cooked and pink.

3. Remove from oven, sprinkle with parsley and lemon juice, and toss to combine.

Easy-peasy Chicken Parm

Chicken Parmigiana is a favorite dish of my niece and great-grandgirls, often ordered when they eat out. Now, with this quick and simple recipe, they can make a similar dish at home. Extra tomato sauce might be requested. Serve with a salad or cooked spaghetti, or both.

MAKES 3 SERVINGS

2 cups	homemade or storebought tomato sauce, divided	500 mL
1 lb	frozen breaded chicken breast strips or nuggets	500 g
1 cup	grated mozzarella cheese, divided	250 mL
¼ cup	grated Parmesan cheese	50 mL

1. Spoon 1 cup (250 mL) tomato sauce into a greased 8-inch (2 L) square baking dish. Arrange chicken pieces over sauce, then half the mozzarella, then remaining tomato sauce. Top with remaining mozzarella and Parmesan.

2. Bake in preheated 375°F (190°C) toaster oven for 28 to 30 minutes, or until sauce is bubbling, cheese is melted and internal temperature of chicken is 170°F (75°C).

Purchasing Frozen Breaded Chicken

When purchasing frozen breaded chicken, check labels closely, as some are uncooked and others cooked. Either works, but be sure to check the internal temperature at the end of the baking time to ensure chicken is thoroughly cooked.

Chicken and Noodle Bowl

One-bowl meals are quick to assemble and satisfying as a lunch or light dinner. Leftover cooked chicken (to replace the uncooked chicken breast) can be stirred in with the noodles and snow peas. Most instant noodle packages come with a soup packet. I leave these out, preferring to season my own dish. For a more Asian and spicier version, add hot or sweet chili sauce to taste. These flavors remind me of noodle bowls I savored while touring Thailand.

MAKES 2 TO 3 SERVINGS

Variation

Tofu and Noodle Bowl
Replace chicken stock with vegetable stock. Replace chicken with 1 cup (250 mL) diced firm tofu.

8 oz	boneless, skinless chicken breast, finely diced (about 1 cup/250 mL)	250 g
1	stalk celery, chopped	1
1 cup	grated or finely chopped carrot	250 mL
2 tsp	finely chopped gingerroot	10 mL
2½ cups	chicken stock	625 mL
1 tbsp	soy sauce	15 mL
½ cup	snow peas, trimmed and halved crosswise	125 mL
½ cup	sliced mushrooms	125 mL
2	green onions, chopped	2
1	3- to 3½-oz (85 to 100 g) package instant noodles, broken up	1
2 tbsp	chopped fresh cilantro or parsley	25 mL
1 tbsp	lime juice	15 mL

1. In a 6-cup (1.5 L) ovenproof bowl or an 8-inch (2 L) square ovenproof glass baking dish, combine chicken, celery, carrot, ginger, stock and soy sauce.

2. Bake in preheated 400°F (200°C) toaster oven for 25 minutes, or until stock is very hot and bubbling at edges. Vegetables will still be very crunchy and chicken will be almost cooked.

3. Carefully remove dish from oven (it will be hot). Stir in snow peas, mushrooms, green onions and noodles.

4. Return to oven and continue to bake for 10 to 12 minutes, or until stock is again bubbling at edges and chicken is no longer pink inside.

5. Remove from oven and stir in cilantro and lime juice. Serve in soup bowls.

Homemade Chicken Fingers

Homemade chicken fingers require some preparation, but these are worth the effort. Many supermarkets now offer pre-sliced chicken breasts, which are perfect for this dish. Serve with a favorite dipping sauce, especially for children — they love dipping their food.

MAKES 3 SERVINGS

Variation

For a gluten-free version, replace flour with a gluten-free flour, and breadcrumbs with corn flake crumbs, gluten-free breadcrumbs or cracker crumbs.

½ cup	all-purpose flour	125 mL
½ tsp	salt	2 mL
¼ tsp	black pepper	1 mL
2	eggs, beaten with 1 tbsp (15 mL) water	2
¾ cup	seasoned dry breadcrumbs or panko	175 mL
¼ cup	grated Parmesan cheese	50 mL
1 lb	chicken tenders or boneless, skinless chicken breasts, cut into strips (about 10 pieces)	500 g
2 tbsp	olive oil or melted butter, divided	25 mL

1. On a shallow plate with a rim, combine flour, salt and pepper. Pour egg wash onto a second plate. Combine breadcrumbs and cheese on a third plate.

2. Dip chicken pieces on both sides in flour mixture, then into beaten egg, shaking off excess. Roll in breadcrumb mixture, pressing crumbs in lightly. Discard any excess flour mixture, egg wash and breadcrumb mixture.

3. Brush parchment- or foil-lined oven pan with half the oil. Arrange breaded chicken in a single layer, without crowding pieces. Drizzle with remaining oil.

4. Bake in preheated 400°F (200°C) toaster oven for 20 to 25 minutes, turning partway through, until golden and no longer pink inside.

Panko

Breadcrumbs are the typical breading ingredient, but if panko is available, use it. These Japanese breadcrumbs used to be hard to find but are now available in most supermarkets. If panko is unavailable, use seasoned dry breadcrumbs.

Craig's Roast Beef and Cheese Sliders

My nephew Craig often prepares these sliders for a casual supper, using leftovers from their family roast beef dinner. He uses prepared roasted garlic mayonnaise (also called spread). If this is unavailable, combine mayonnaise with garlic powder to taste. If there is leftover gravy or juices from the roast, serve it for dipping.

MAKES 3 TO 4 SERVINGS

Variation

Replace garlic mayonnaise with another flavored mayonnaise (or spread), such as Sriracha mayonnaise or chipotle mayonnaise.

8	soft dinner rolls, split	8
3 tbsp	garlic mayonnaise	45 mL
8	slices deli or leftover roast beef	8
8	slices provolone cheese	8
¼	Spanish or sweet onion, thinly sliced (optional)	¼
¼ cup	melted butter	50 mL
2 tsp	sesame or poppy seeds (optional)	10 mL

1. Arrange bottom halves of dinner rolls on foil- or parchment-lined oven pan. Spread with half the mayonnaise. Top with beef, cheese and onion, if using. Spread remaining mayonnaise over top halves of dinner rolls and place tops over filling. Brush tops with butter and sprinkle with sesame seeds, if using.

2. Bake in preheated 350°F (180°C) toaster oven for 10 to 12 minutes, or until cheese oozes out slightly and tops are golden.

Oven-baked Sloppy Joes

Sloppy Joes are a favorite with all ages. For lunch, just serve fresh vegetable pieces on the side. For supper, add Cabbage and Carrot Slaw (page 95) to the menu. Rather than using the traditional rolls, try serving the meat mixture with steamed rice, or offer warmed tortillas or lettuce leaves and let everyone make their own wrap.

MAKES 3 TO 4 SERVINGS

Make Ahead

Sloppy Joes can be made a day ahead, covered and refrigerated. Reheat, covered, in preheated 350°F (180°C) toaster oven for 20 minutes, stirring occasionally, until hot.

Variation

Sloppy Joe Chili

Add 1 cup (250 mL) rinsed drained canned black beans and 1 tsp (5 mL) chili powder to the meat mixture.

1 lb	extra-lean ground beef, chicken or turkey	500 g
1 cup	tomato sauce	250 mL
½ cup	ketchup	125 mL
1 tbsp	dried onion flakes, or ¼ cup (50 mL) chopped onion	15 mL
1 tsp	dried oregano leaves	5 mL
½ tsp	salt	2 mL
¼ tsp	black pepper	1 mL
¼ tsp	hot red pepper flakes	1 mL
4	crusty rolls	4

1. In a 6-cup (1.5 L) casserole or baking dish, combine beef, tomato sauce, ketchup, onion flakes, oregano, salt, black pepper and hot pepper flakes.

2. Bake, uncovered, in preheated 350°F (180°C) toaster oven for 35 to 40 minutes, stirring occasionally, until meat is no longer pink and mixture is bubbling. Mixture will be a bit "sloppy."

3. Remove casserole from oven and heat rolls in toaster oven for 4 to 5 minutes. Split rolls and spoon meat mixture onto bottom halves. Cover with top halves of rolls.

The Ranch Beef Burger

Since I don't have a barbecue now, I cook my burgers in the toaster oven, sometimes brushing them with Barbecue Sauce (page 73) towards the end of the cooking time. A bonus is that you can cook them with add-ons (see Variations: Mushrooms and Onions) along with the burgers. Ground chicken or turkey can be substituted for beef.

MAKES 2 TO 4 SERVINGS

Variations

Mushrooms and Onions
Combine 1 thinly sliced onion, 1½ cups (375 mL) sliced mushrooms and 2 tsp (10 mL) olive oil. Arrange around burger patties on pan, stirring once during baking.

Peppers and Onions
Combine ½ cup (125 mL) each diced red bell pepper and diced red onion. Spoon over burger patties during last 5 minutes of baking.

Cheeseburgers
Top each burger patty with a slice of your favorite cheese, such as Cheddar, Monterey Jack or even crumbled blue cheese, during the last 3 minutes of baking.

Avocado, Tomato and Lettuce
Top each burger patty with avocado slices, tomato slices and lettuce leaves before serving.

1 lb	extra-lean or lean ground beef	500 g
¼ cup	seasoned dry breadcrumbs	50 mL
½ tsp	salt	2 mL
¼ tsp	black pepper	1 mL
1	egg, beaten	1
1 tsp	mustard (Dijon or prepared)	5 mL
1 tsp	Worcestershire or soy sauce	5 mL
4	hamburger or kaiser rolls, split	4

1. In a large bowl, combine beef, breadcrumbs, salt, pepper, egg, mustard and Worcestershire sauce. Shape into four 4-inch (10 cm) flattish patties.

2. Place patties on parchment- or foil-lined oven pan. (Bring parchment paper or foil up the sides of the pan, but not hanging over the sides. This protects the pan and makes for easy cleanup.)

3. Bake in preheated 375°F (190°C) toaster oven for 25 to 28 minutes, turning once, until no longer pink inside. Serve on your favorite rolls.

BBQ Meatballs

Few people can walk by a platter of meatballs. They are a snacking food as well as part of a meal. Serve as an appetizer, with mashed potatoes and a salad as a main course, or with kettle chips, rolls and pickles as sides.

MAKES 4 SERVINGS

Make Ahead

Meatballs can be made a day ahead, covered and refrigerated overnight. Add ¼ cup (50 mL) water to the baking dish and reheat, covered with foil, in preheated 350°F (180°C) toaster oven for 20 minutes, or until heated through.

1 lb	extra-lean ground beef, chicken or turkey	500 g
¼ cup	finely chopped onion	50 mL
¼ cup	grated Parmesan cheese (optional)	50 mL
¼ cup	dry breadcrumbs (plain or seasoned)	50 mL
½ tsp	salt	2 mL
¼ tsp	black pepper	1 mL
1	egg, beaten	1
1 tbsp	Worcestershire sauce	15 mL
1 cup	homemade or storebought barbecue sauce	250 mL
¼ cup	water	50 mL

1. In a large bowl, combine beef, onion, Parmesan, if using, breadcrumbs, salt, pepper, egg and Worcestershire sauce. Shape mixture into about 25 meatballs, about 1 inch (2.5 cm) in diameter. Arrange in a lightly greased 8-inch (2 L) square baking dish.

2. Combine barbecue sauce and water. Pour over meatballs.

3. Bake in preheated 375°F (190°C) toaster oven for 35 to 37 minutes, stirring gently a few times to coat meatballs with sauce, until meatballs are no longer pink inside.

Baked Ham and Pineapple

When a large bone-in ham is more than you need, switch to a smaller prepared ham and bake it with pineapple pieces. Quick to assemble, the ham can be baking while you prepare mashed potatoes and coleslaw to go alongside. Cold leftover ham is great for sandwiches or with Hash Brown Gratin (page 135). If you prefer just a few pineapple pieces, reserve the rest, along with the remaining juice, for a smoothie.

MAKES 4 TO 5 SERVINGS

1	boneless smoked ham (about 1½ lbs/ 750 g)	1
⅓ cup	packed brown sugar	75 mL
2 tsp	Dijon mustard	10 mL
1	14-oz (398 mL) can pineapple chunks, drained, juice reserved	1

1. Cut ham in half lengthwise. Cut each half into serving slices (about 10 slices per side). Arrange slices, overlapping, in a lightly greased 8-inch (2 L) square baking dish.
2. In a small bowl, combine brown sugar, mustard and ⅓ cup (75 mL) reserved pineapple juice. Spoon over ham.
3. Bake in preheated 375°F (190°C) toaster oven for 25 minutes, or until sauce is bubbling.
4. Remove from oven and spoon pineapple pieces on top of ham.
5. Return to oven and continue to bake for 15 minutes, or until pineapple pieces are heated through.
6. Serve from baking dish or, using tongs or a slotted spoon, transfer to a serving platter and arrange pineapple chunks over ham.

Roasted Oktoberfest Sausages

Many types of sausages are readily available in supermarkets. Besides Oktoberfest, other varieties include Italian, honey garlic, apple sage and bratwurst. Sausages vary in size. Some are long, while others are more pudgy. Generally, a sausage weighs about 4 oz (125 g). Because of the variation, roasting times may need to be adjusted slightly. When cooking sausages as the main part of a meal, I often add a vegetable or baked beans and serve with a green salad. If there are any leftover sausages, add them to pasta or even use them in a sandwich.

MAKES 2 TO 3 SERVINGS

| 12 oz | Oktoberfest or other favorite sausages (about 3) | 375 g |

1. Arrange sausages on parchment- or foil-lined oven pan, spacing them apart so they brown properly. Roast in preheated 350°F (180°C) toaster oven for 25 to 30 minutes, turning once, until juices run clear when sausages are pierced with the tip of a sharp knife.

Sausages and Sweet Potatoes

Peel 2 medium sweet potatoes (each about 8 oz/250 g). Cut into ¾-inch (2 cm) pieces. Toss with 2 tsp (10 mL) olive or vegetable oil and some salt and pepper. Arrange sweet potatoes around sausages and roast for 33 to 35 minutes, turning two or three times, until potatoes are tender and sausages are golden.

Sausages with Mini Potatoes

Cut 1 lb (500 g) mini potatoes in half (or into quarters, if large). Toss with 2 tsp (10 mL) olive or vegetable oil and some salt and pepper. Arrange potatoes around sausages and roast for 33 to 35 minutes, turning a few times, until potatoes are tender and sausages are golden.

Sausages with Baked Beans

Arrange sausages in an 8-inch (2 L) square baking dish. Bake for 25 to 28 minutes, or until starting to brown and almost cooked. Stir in a 14-oz (398 mL) can of baked beans, ¼ cup (50 mL) ketchup, chili sauce or tomato sauce, and ½ tsp (2 mL) garlic or onion powder. Continue to bake for 20 to 25 minutes, or until beans are bubbling and hot.

One-dish Spaghetti with Sausage and Feta

Sausage meat is already seasoned, so you don't need to add a lot of extra seasonings yourself. If you keep the meat in larger pieces, it will sort of be like small meatballs. When this is served right away, the dish is almost soup-like. Serve with crusty bread and a Caesar salad.

MAKES 3 SERVINGS

Make Ahead

The dish can be baked a day ahead, covered and refrigerated. It will thicken on cooling. Stir in $1/3$ cup (75 mL) water, cover and reheat in preheated 325°F (160°C) toaster oven for 20 to 25 minutes, stirring occasionally, until heated through. If too thick, stir in more water.

12 oz	Italian sausage meat (removed from casings)	375 g
1¼ cups	broken-up uncooked spaghetti	300 mL
½ cup	crumbled feta cheese	125 mL
½ tsp	dried oregano leaves	2 mL
¼ tsp	black pepper	1 mL
1½ cups	tomato pasta sauce	375 mL
1½ cups	water	375 mL

1. In a large bowl, combine sausage meat, spaghetti pieces, feta, oregano, pepper, tomato sauce and water.

2. Spoon sausage mixture into a greased 8-inch (2 L) square ovenproof glass baking dish. Cover with foil.

3. Bake in preheated 400°F (200°C) toaster oven for 40 to 45 minutes, stirring two to three times, until spaghetti is tender. Let stand for 5 minutes before serving.

Vegetable Bean Chili

There are never enough chili recipes and ideas. This quick and easy version is a substantial one-dish meal. Serve condiments alongside, such as chopped fresh cilantro, chopped green onion, corn chips or sour cream. Cornbread (page 167) is an excellent accompaniment that can be prepared ahead.

MAKES 3 SERVINGS

Make Ahead

Chili can be prepared a day ahead, covered and refrigerated. Reheat, covered, in preheated 375°F (190°C) toaster oven for 25 minutes, stirring a few times, until hot.

2	cloves garlic, minced	2
1	small onion, chopped	1
1	stalk celery, chopped	1
1	small zucchini, diced	1
1	red bell pepper, seeded and diced	1
1	19-oz (540 mL) can stewed tomatoes, chopped	1
1 cup	fresh or frozen corn kernels	250 mL
1 cup	rinsed drained canned black beans or chickpeas	250 mL
1 cup	tomato juice or tomato sauce	250 mL
1½ tsp	chili powder	7 mL
½ tsp	dried oregano leaves	2 mL
½ tsp	salt	2 mL
¼ tsp	black pepper	1 mL

1. In an 8-cup (2 L) shallow casserole or baking dish, combine garlic, onion, celery, zucchini, red pepper, tomatoes, corn, beans, tomato juice, chili powder, oregano, salt and pepper.

2. Bake, covered, in preheated 400°F (200°C) toaster oven for 35 minutes. Remove cover and bake for 20 minutes, or until celery and zucchini are tender and chili is bubbling. Stir a few times during cooking.

Canned Beans and Tomatoes

In some supermarkets, small cans (7½ oz/213 mL) of beans and chickpeas are available; if using larger cans, use leftovers in soups or salads. A variety of stewed tomatoes with different seasonings is available; choose your favorite.

Baked "Fries"

These are not traditional fries. They are baked and are jumbo-size. I sometimes make them as a snack to share, when I want something more substantial than a celery stick, but I don't make this a habit. I serve them with vinegar and ketchup.

MAKES 2 SERVINGS

2	large baking potatoes	2
1½ tbsp	olive oil	22 mL
¾ tsp	salt or other seasonings (see box)	4 mL
¼ tsp	black pepper	1 mL

About Salt and Seasonings

Many types of salt are now widely available. Kosher salt is mild, with small crystals, and is not as salty as regular table salt. If you have it, try it. A wide variety of mixed seasonings, often used for meat, fish and poultry, is available in the spice section. Try one of these in place of salt. Do not use both, or the potatoes will be too salty.

1. Cut potatoes in half lengthwise, then cut each half lengthwise into 4 wedges. Place on parchment-lined oven pan. Add oil, salt and pepper, toss and turn potatoes to coat with oil, then arrange in a single layer, with a cut side down.
2. Bake in preheated 400°F (200°C) toaster oven for 35 to 40 minutes, turning after 20 minutes onto another cut side, until potatoes are tender and golden brown. (Timing depends on size of wedges.) Transfer to serving dishes. Potatoes will be very hot.

Baked Sweet Potatoes

In Scotland, baked potato restaurants are everywhere, and are very popular. Besides the traditional toppings of butter and sour cream, serve these potatoes with salsa or chili.

MAKES 2 SERVINGS

2	medium sweet potatoes	2
2 tsp	olive or vegetable oil	10 mL
½ tsp	salt	2 mL

1. Cut sweet potatoes in half lengthwise. Brush cut sides with oil. Sprinkle with salt. Place on parchment- or foil-lined oven pan, with the cut side up.
2. Bake in preheated 400°F (200°C) toaster oven for 30 to 35 minutes, or until fork-tender.

Oven-roasted Mixed Veggies

This colorful vegetable combination is a snap to prepare. If I have any leftovers, I include them in a salad for lunch. Baby potatoes can be replaced with sweet potatoes, cut in ½-inch (1 cm) pieces. Serve with cold roast chicken (page 72), cold ham (page 23) or deli meats.

MAKES 2 TO 3 SERVINGS

8 oz	baby potatoes, halved (quartered if largish)	250 g
1 tbsp	olive oil	15 mL
½ tsp	salt	2 mL
¼ tsp	black pepper	1 mL
1	small zucchini, halved lengthwise and cut in ½-inch (1 cm) pieces	1
½	red bell pepper, seeded and cut in ½-inch (1 cm) pieces	½
8 oz	thin asparagus, tough ends removed, cut in 2-inch (5 cm) lengths	250 g
4 oz	green beans, trimmed and halved crosswise	125 g

1. Arrange potatoes on parchment- or foil-lined oven pan. Add oil, salt and pepper, toss and turn potatoes to coat with oil, then arrange in a single layer. Roast in preheated 425°F (220°C) toaster oven for 12 minutes.

2. Add zucchini, red pepper, asparagus and green beans to oven pan. Toss to coat all vegetables with oil. Roast for 15 to 18 minutes, or until all vegetables are tender.

Brunch Quiche

Quiche is such a versatile dish, perfect for a weekend brunch, for lunch or for supper. Pair it with a crunchy salad to round out the meal.

MAKES 4 TO 6 SERVINGS

Variation

Spinach and Cheddar Quiche

Omit ham. Defrost ¾ cup (175 mL) frozen spinach and squeeze out excess moisture. Sprinkle over bottom of baked pie shell, then gently spoon egg mixture on top. Frozen spinach is available loose, so you don't have to defrost a whole package.

Deep-Dish Pie Shells

Frozen deep-dish pie shells are available in the frozen pastry section. Follow package directions for baking. Be sure to purchase the deep-dish shells, as pastry has a tendency to shrink a bit when baking.

2	eggs	2
¾ cup	milk or cream	175 mL
1 cup	grated Cheddar cheese	250 mL
¾ cup	diced cooked ham or turkey	175 mL
1 tsp	dried dillweed, or 1 tbsp (15 mL) chopped fresh	5 mL
¼ tsp	salt	1 mL
¼ tsp	black pepper	1 mL
Pinch	ground nutmeg (optional)	Pinch
1	baked 9-inch (23 cm) deep-dish pie shell	1

1. In a large bowl, beat eggs until just combined. Stir in milk, cheese, ham, dill, salt, pepper and nutmeg, if using.

2. Gently pour egg mixture into baked pie shell and carefully distribute cheese and ham evenly.

3. Bake in preheated 350°F (180°C) toaster oven for 45 minutes, or until center is set. If quiche is browning too much on one side, turn halfway through baking time. Let stand for 10 minutes before serving.

Oven Omelet

In a large bowl, beat together 6 eggs, ½ cup (125 mL) milk and ½ tsp (2 mL) salt. Stir in 2 chopped green onions and ½ cup (125 mL) grated Cheddar cheese. If desired, add ½ cup (125 mL) of any of the following: diced cooked ham, cooked bacon or sausage, diced cooked potato or cooked corn, and/or ¼ cup (50 mL) chopped red or green bell pepper. Grease a 9-inch (23 cm) glass pie plate with 2 tsp (10 mL) olive oil or softened butter. Pour in egg mixture. Bake in preheated 350°F (180°C) toaster oven for 25 minutes or until just firm in center. Remove from oven and let stand for 3 to 4 minutes. Cut into serving pieces. Makes 2 to 3 servings.

Cottage Ham and Eggs

When I visit my great quilting friend/mentor Helen Fujiki at her cottage, she always makes these, as she knows they are among my favorites. While they are baking, she puts the coffee on to brew and quickly assembles a fruit plate. She's very organized.

MAKES 3 TO 6 SERVINGS

Variation

Replace tomato salsa with 1 tsp (5 mL) homemade or storebought pesto per muffin cup.

6	thin slices deli ham, without holes	6
6 tbsp	grated Tex-Mex blend or Cheddar cheese	90 mL
6 tbsp	tomato salsa	90 mL
6	eggs	6
	Salt and black pepper	
3	English muffins, split	3

1. Lightly grease a 6-cup muffin pan. Line each cup with a ham slice. Spoon in 1 tbsp (15 mL) cheese and 1 tbsp (15 mL) salsa. Carefully break an egg into each cup. Sprinkle with salt and pepper.

2. Bake in preheated 400°F (200°C) toaster oven for 12 to 15 minutes, or until eggs reach desired doneness.

3. Remove muffin pan from oven and immediately toast muffin halves. Using a narrow silicone spatula, gently remove ham and eggs from pan and serve on toasted muffins.

Carrot Muffins

Carrot muffins make a great snacking food to wrap and pack in lunches, or to eat on the go. These are less cakey than many storebought or takeout muffins. Olive oil has become quite popular for baking in place of vegetable oil or melted butter. If using it, choose a mild-flavored one.

MAKES 6 MUFFINS

Make Ahead

Muffins can be baked, wrapped individually, packaged and frozen for up to 3 weeks.

1¼ cups	all-purpose flour	300 mL
½ cup	packed brown sugar	125 mL
1 tsp	ground cinnamon	5 mL
1 tsp	baking powder	5 mL
½ tsp	baking soda	2 mL
¼ tsp	salt	1 mL
1	egg	1
½ cup	olive oil, vegetable oil or melted butter	125 mL
¼ cup	orange or apple juice	50 mL
1¼ cups	grated carrots	300 mL
¼ cup	sunflower seeds (optional)	50 mL

1. In a large bowl, combine flour, brown sugar, cinnamon, baking powder, baking soda and salt.

2. In a separate bowl, beat egg. Stir in oil and orange juice. Add to dry ingredients, along with carrot and sunflower seeds, if using. Stir just to combine. Spoon batter into six lightly greased muffin cups.

3. Bake in preheated 375°F (190°C) toaster oven for 23 to 25 minutes, or until muffin tops are firm to the touch. Turn pan halfway through baking time. Cool muffins in pan for 5 minutes before turning out onto a rack.

Small-batch Oatmeal Raisin Cookies

My local bakery reports that oatmeal raisin cookies are their best seller. For variety, the raisins are sometimes replaced with dried cranberries, chocolate chips or chopped pecans. Pack these with your lunch or just enjoy one with hot chocolate on a blustery winter day — or anytime! These cookies freeze well.

MAKES ABOUT 15 COOKIES

Make Ahead

Store baked cookies in freezer bags or airtight containers at room temperature for up to 2 weeks or in the freezer for up to 6 months.

¼ cup	butter, softened	50 mL
¼ cup	packed brown sugar	50 mL
1	egg, beaten	1
½ tsp	vanilla	2 mL
½ cup	all-purpose flour	125 mL
½ cup	large-flake rolled oats (not instant)	125 mL
½ tsp	baking soda	2 mL
½ tsp	ground cinnamon	2 mL
¼ tsp	salt	1 mL
½ cup	raisins	125 mL

1. In a large bowl, cream butter and brown sugar until light and fluffy. Beat in egg and vanilla.

2. In a separate bowl, combine flour, oats, baking soda, cinnamon and salt. Add to egg mixture along with raisins. Stir until ingredients are well mixed.

3. Drop 8 mounds of dough in 1 tbsp (15 mL) measures onto parchment-lined or lightly greased oven pan. Flatten slightly with back of a fork dipped in granulated sugar.

4. Bake on inverted bottom rack in preheated 350°F (180°C) toaster oven for 10 to 12 minutes, or until just firm to the touch. Turn pan halfway through baking time. Let cool on pan for 5 minutes before transferring to a rack. Refrigerate or freeze remaining dough or continue to bake batches until all dough is used.

Freezing Cookie Dough

Freeze extra dough in mounds on a baking sheet until firm, then transfer mounds to an airtight container and freeze for up to 2 weeks. Defrost slightly before baking, adding 2 minutes to the baking time.

Small-batch Chocolate Chip Cookies

My family always flocks to a plate of these cookies. They (the cookies) sometimes make an appearance in birthday and Christmas gifts, often by special request. Some like them with chopped walnuts, others without. Of course, these can be frozen (to take for snacks or lunches), but they rarely make it to the freezer.

MAKES 16 TO 18 COOKIES

¼ cup	butter, softened	50 mL
¼ cup	packed brown sugar	50 mL
2 tbsp	granulated sugar	25 mL
1	egg, beaten	1
½ tsp	vanilla	2 mL
¾ cup + 2 tbsp	all-purpose flour	200 mL
½ tsp	baking soda	2 mL
¼ tsp	salt	1 mL
¾ cup	semisweet chocolate chips	175 mL
⅓ cup	chopped walnuts (optional)	75 mL

1. In a large bowl, cream butter and both sugars until light and fluffy. Beat in egg and vanilla.

2. In a separate bowl, combine flour, baking soda and salt. Add to egg mixture along with chocolate chips and walnuts, if using. Stir until ingredients are well mixed. (If mixture is very soft, refrigerate for 20 minutes.)

3. Drop 6 mounds of dough in 1 tbsp (15 mL) measures onto parchment-lined or lightly greased oven pan.

4. Bake on inverted bottom rack in preheated 350°F (180°C) toaster oven for 9 to 11 minutes, or until lightly browned but still slightly soft in the center. Turn pan halfway through baking time. Let cool on pan for 5 minutes before transferring to a rack. Refrigerate or freeze remaining dough or continue to bake batches until all dough is used.

S'mores

From the campfire to the kitchen, these delectable treats can be made any time of the year — no need to wait for camping days. They are a bit messy, so serve with wet wipes.

MAKES 4 SERVINGS

16	single graham wafers (about 2½ inches/ 6 cm square)	16
8	thin squares milk or semisweet chocolate	8
8	large marshmallows	8

1. Arrange 8 single graham wafers on foil- or parchment-lined oven tray. Top each with a chocolate square and a marshmallow.

2. Bake in preheated 400°F (200°C) toaster oven for 5 to 6 minutes, or until chocolate is softened and marshmallow is softened, slightly golden and starting to flatten.

3. Remove tray from oven and top each s'more with one of the remaining single graham wafers. Carefully transfer to serving dishes. Press to partially flatten and let chocolate and marshmallow ooze out the sides.

Appetizers and Snacks

Shrimp with Pesto and Prosciutto

This is an elegant appetizer that takes just minutes to prepare. Serve these shrimp hot or warm, as a starter or on toothpicks as finger food. If you wish, you can omit the prosciutto (reduce the cooking time by a minute or so).

MAKES 3 TO 4 SERVINGS

15	large shrimp, peeled and deveined	15
3 tbsp	basil pesto (page 63)	45 mL
5	thin slices prosciutto	5

Make Ahead

Shrimp can be prepared, covered and refrigerated up to 4 hours before baking.

Variation

Scallops with Pesto and Prosciutto

Use 15 large scallops (about 1 lb/500 g) instead of shrimp. Bake for 8 minutes, or until scallops are opaque.

1. Pat shrimp dry and place in a large bowl. Add pesto and toss until shrimp are coated.
2. Cut each prosciutto slice lengthwise into 3 pieces. Wrap each shrimp with prosciutto, tucking in ends.
3. Place shrimp, seam side down, in a single layer on lightly greased oven pan.
4. Bake in preheated 400°F (200°C) toaster oven for 8 minutes, or until shrimp are cooked and pink.

Peeling and Deveining Shrimp

Gently peel the shell from the body of the shrimp, carefully breaking the shell and easing it off, leaving the tail intact. With a sharp knife, make a slit down the back of the shrimp and pull out the "vein" (intestinal tract). Rinse the shrimp in cold water.

Garlic Shrimp and Mushrooms

The flavors in this dish remind me of escargots in garlic butter. Serve it in scallop shells as a starter with French baguette.

MAKES 4 SERVINGS

1 lb	shrimp, peeled and deveined (see box, page 36)	500 g
3 cups	quartered mushrooms (about 8 oz/250 g)	750 mL
1/4 cup	olive oil	50 mL
1/4 cup	chopped fresh parsley	50 mL
1/4 cup	fresh breadcrumbs	50 mL
2 tbsp	grated Parmesan cheese	25 mL
4	cloves garlic, minced	4
1/2 tsp	paprika	2 mL
1/2 tsp	salt	2 mL
1/4 tsp	black pepper	1 mL

1. Pat shrimp dry.
2. In a large bowl, combine shrimp, mushrooms, oil, parsley, breadcrumbs, Parmesan, garlic, paprika, salt and pepper. Spoon into an 8-inch (2 L) square baking dish.
3. Bake in preheated 400°F (200°C) toaster oven for 25 minutes, or just until shrimp are pink and cooked. Stir twice during cooking.

Coconut Shrimp

This favorite cooks nicely in the toaster oven instead of being deep-fried as it is traditionally. Serve it with the dipping sauce or with sweet Asian chili sauce.

MAKES 3 TO 4 SERVINGS

1	egg white	1
1 tbsp	cornstarch	15 mL
2 tsp	soy sauce	10 mL
¾ cup	shredded coconut	175 mL
12 oz	large shrimp (about 24), peeled and deveined (see box, page 36)	375 g

Dipping Sauce

3 tbsp	lime juice or lemon juice	45 mL
2 tbsp	water	25 mL
1 tbsp	fish sauce	15 mL
1 tbsp	granulated sugar	15 mL
½ tsp	roasted sesame oil	2 mL
1	clove garlic, minced	1
Pinch	hot red pepper flakes	Pinch

1. In a shallow dish, using a fork or mini whisk, beat together egg white, cornstarch and soy sauce. Place coconut in a separate shallow dish.

2. Holding shrimp by the tail, roll in egg white mixture. Let excess drip off, then roll in coconut to coat.

3. Arrange shrimp in a single layer on lightly greased broiler rack placed over oven pan. Bake in preheated 400°F (200°C) toaster oven for 15 minutes, or until shrimp is opaque and coconut is toasted.

4. Meanwhile, to prepare dipping sauce, in a small bowl or measuring cup, combine lime juice, water, fish sauce, sugar, sesame oil, garlic and hot pepper flakes. Transfer sauce to a small bowl or individual dishes and serve with shrimp.

Sesame Oil

Roasted sesame oil is a rich, nutty oil made from roasted sesame seeds. It is used sparingly as a seasoning. Buy the Asian version rather than the unroasted sesame oil found in Middle Eastern stores or health food stores. Refrigerate after opening.

Salmon Satays

You'll only need a small amount of salmon to make this special-occasion appetizer. Most stores now sell salmon fillets in 6-oz (175 g) portions, making it easy to assemble these ribbon-like satays. They can be served hot or cold.

MAKES 6 APPETIZERS (2 TO 3 SERVINGS)

Variation

Chicken Satays
In place of salmon, use thin strips of chicken tenderloin or boneless, skinless chicken breast. Broil satays for an extra minute, or until chicken is no longer pink.

2 tbsp	plum sauce	25 mL
2 tbsp	oyster sauce	25 mL
2 tsp	lemon juice or lime juice	10 mL
1 tsp	finely chopped gingerroot	5 mL
1	clove garlic, minced	1
1	6-oz (175 g) salmon fillet, skin removed	1
1 tsp	sesame seeds (optional)	5 mL

1. To make marinade, in a small bowl or measuring cup, combine plum sauce, oyster sauce, lemon juice, ginger and garlic.
2. Cut salmon lengthwise into 6 strips. Thread salmon onto six 6- to 8-inch (15 to 20 cm) bamboo skewers.
3. Spoon marinade over both sides of salmon.
4. Arrange satays on lightly greased broiler rack placed over oven pan, with exposed skewer ends near oven door to prevent burning.
5. Broil under preheated toaster oven broiler for 2 minutes per side, or just until white juices rise to surface. Turn carefully. Sprinkle with sesame seeds, if using, during last 30 seconds of cooking.

Roasted Peppers with Caper Tapenade

Roasted red peppers are a favorite item on many Mediterranean-style menus, and they are so easy to prepare in the toaster oven. Serve these as part of an antipasto course (they are best served with forks).

Tapenade, traditionally based on olives, receives a boost here with extra capers and mint. It can also be served separately as a dip, pasta sauce, or as a sauce for baked fish or chicken.

MAKES 12 PIECES (4 TO 6 SERVINGS)

Make Ahead

Peppers and tapenade can be prepared, covered and refrigerated a day ahead. Dish can be assembled up to 2 hours before serving.

3	red bell peppers, seeded and quartered	3
1 tbsp	olive oil	15 mL
Caper Tapenade		
1/3 cup	pitted black or green olives	75 mL
1/4 cup	drained capers	50 mL
2	anchovy fillets	2
2 tbsp	coarsely chopped oil-packed sun-dried tomatoes	25 mL
1	clove garlic, coarsely chopped	1
1/3 cup	packed mint leaves	75 mL
2 tbsp	olive oil	25 mL

1. Arrange peppers cut side up in a single layer on lightly greased oven pan. Brush with olive oil.

2. Bake in preheated 400°F (200°C) toaster oven for 25 minutes, or until tender and starting to color. Remove and arrange on a serving platter. Cool.

3. Meanwhile, to prepare tapenade, place olives, capers, anchovies, sun-dried tomatoes, garlic and mint in food processor. Puree until coarse.

4. Add olive oil to food processor and puree until smooth.

5. Spoon tapenade into center of each baked pepper piece. Serve at room temperature.

Mediterranean Stuffed Mushrooms

Serve these as a starter or as a side dish with fish or poultry. If jumbo mushrooms are unavailable, just use more of the smaller ones. To prevent the mushrooms from wobbling, cut a small slice off the tops so they will sit flat when upside-down. Six medium-sized portobello mushrooms could also be substituted.

MAKES 5 TO 6 SERVINGS

10 to 12	jumbo mushrooms, stemmed (about 2½ inches/7 cm in diameter)	10 to 12
¾ cup	cooked brown or white rice	175 mL
2 tbsp	chopped oil-packed sun-dried tomatoes	25 mL
1	clove garlic, minced	1
2	green onions, finely chopped	2
2 tbsp	chopped fresh dillweed	25 mL
2 tbsp	chopped fresh parsley	25 mL
½ cup	crumbled feta cheese (about 3 oz/90 g)	125 mL
½ tsp	salt	2 mL
¼ tsp	black pepper	1 mL
¼ cup	dried currants (optional)	50 mL
2 tbsp	olive oil	25 mL
2 tbsp	lemon juice	25 mL

1. Arrange mushrooms stem side up in a single layer on oven pan.

2. To prepare filling, in a bowl, combine rice, sun-dried tomatoes, garlic, green onions, dill, parsley, feta, salt, pepper and currants, if using. Spoon filling into mushroom caps, mounding in center.

3. In a small measuring cup, combine olive oil and lemon juice. Drizzle over mushrooms.

4. Bake in preheated 350°F (180°C) toaster oven for 15 to 18 minutes, or until mushrooms are cooked and filling is hot. Let stand for 2 minutes before serving.

Onion and Olive Pizzettes

Onions are the workhorse vegetable, used as the base for many dishes. But they can also be the main attraction, as in these little pizzettes, which are similar to pissaladière, the Provençal version of pizza. The onions are cooked until they are golden and sweet.

Peeling onions leaves some cooks in tears. Over the years I have heard of various solutions such as putting the onions in the freezer for 10 minutes (just don't forget them!), wearing swimming or ski goggles, or having friends do the chopping. (Or you can try using sweet onions such as Spanish or Vidalia.) But even if none of these methods works for you, these pizzettes are worth the tears.

You can use crumbled blue cheese or diced Brie (without the rind) in place of the Parmesan or provolone. You can also double or triple the onion topping and make more pizzettes as you need them.

MAKES 2 PIZZETTES (12 PIECES)

Make Ahead		

Prepare onion topping, cover and refrigerate up to 2 days before baking.

2 tbsp	olive oil	25 mL
2	onions, chopped	2
2	cloves garlic, finely chopped	2
1	anchovy fillet, finely chopped, or 1 tsp (5 mL) anchovy paste	1
1/4 tsp	salt	1 mL
1/4 tsp	black pepper	1 mL
1/4 tsp	dried thyme leaves or herbes de Provence	1 mL
2	6-inch (15 cm) flour tortillas	2
1/4 cup	pitted black olives, halved	50 mL
1/4 cup	grated Parmesan or provolone cheese	50 mL

1. In a large skillet, heat oil over medium-high heat. Add onions and garlic. Cook for 8 minutes, or until onions are very soft and golden, stirring frequently near end of cooking time.

2. Stir in anchovy, salt, pepper and thyme.

3. Arrange tortillas on oven pan and prick with a fork to prevent puffing. Spread onion mixture over tortillas. Top with olives and cheese.

4. Bake in preheated 350°F (180°C) toaster oven for 10 to 12 minutes, or until pizzettes are hot and cheese has melted. Cut each pizzette into 6 wedges. Serve warm or at room temperature.

Quickie Pizzas

Make your favorite pizzas using ready-made bases such as pita rounds, storebought pizza bases, flour tortillas (pricked with a fork so they will stay flat) and even crusty bread or rolls. Try some of the following combinations or invent your own.

Place the base on oven pan and spread with topping of your choice. Bake in preheated 400°F (200°C) toaster oven for 8 to 10 minutes, or until base is crisp and topping is heated through.

- **Classic:** Pizza sauce or pasta sauce topped with thinly sliced pepperoni, grated mozzarella cheese and grated Parmesan.
- **Vegetarian:** Hummus, crumbled feta, halved cherry tomatoes and a pinch of dried oregano.
- **Mediterranean:** Roasted red pepper strips (page 40), sliced black or green olives and grated Swiss cheese.
- **California:** Chopped oil-packed sun-dried tomatoes, crumbled chèvre (goat cheese) and shredded arugula.
- **Chicken and Mango:** Diced cooked chicken, chopped red onion, mango chutney and grated Cheddar cheese.
- **Italian:** Pizza sauce or pasta sauce, diced prosciutto, ham or cooked bacon and grated mozzarella cheese.
- **Pesto:** Pesto (page 63), thinly sliced tomato and mozzarella slices.

Crab Melts

This mixture also makes a great sandwich filling. As a substitute for crab, use diced imitation crab or even canned tuna.

MAKES 6 PIECES

Make Ahead

Topping can be prepared, covered and refrigerated up to 8 hours before assembling.

1	7-oz (200 g) package frozen crabmeat, defrosted	1
½ cup	diced Cheddar, Brie or Asiago cheese	125 mL
¼ cup	finely chopped celery	50 mL
¼ cup	finely chopped red bell pepper	50 mL
¼ cup	finely chopped green onion	50 mL
⅓ cup	mayonnaise	75 mL
1 tsp	Russian-style mustard	5 mL
½ tsp	salt	2 mL
¼ tsp	black pepper	1 mL
3	English muffins	3

1. Place crab in a sieve and press gently to squeeze out moisture.
2. In a medium bowl, combine crab, cheese, celery, red pepper, green onion, mayonnaise, mustard, salt and pepper.
3. Cut English muffins in half horizontally. Arrange cut side up on oven pan. Bake in preheated 350°F (180°C) toaster oven for 7 minutes.
4. Spread crab mixture evenly over muffins. Return to oven and bake for 8 to 10 minutes, or until topping is heated through and cheese has melted slightly.

Mushroom Bruschetta

If you love mushrooms, this bruschetta could become a favorite comfort food. The topping can also be used on baked potatoes (page 130).

MAKES 4 LARGE BRUSCHETTA

2 tbsp	olive oil, divided	25 mL
8 oz	mushrooms, sliced	250 g
3	cloves garlic, finely chopped	3
2 tbsp	chopped fresh parsley	25 mL
2 tbsp	chopped fresh basil	25 mL
½ tsp	salt	2 mL
¼ tsp	black pepper	1 mL
½ cup	grated Fontina or Asiago cheese	125 mL
4	slices French or Italian bread, about 1 inch (2.5 cm) thick	4

1. In a large skillet, heat 1 tbsp (15 mL) olive oil over medium-high heat. Add mushrooms and garlic. Cook, stirring occasionally, until mushrooms are golden and moisture has evaporated, about 8 minutes. Spoon into a bowl and let cool for 20 minutes.
2. Stir in parsley, basil, salt, pepper and cheese.
3. Brush both sides of bread with remaining 1 tbsp (15 mL) olive oil. Arrange bread slices on oven pan. Bake in preheated 400°F (200°C) toaster oven for 4 minutes, or until golden.
4. Spoon mushroom mixture over bread slices. Continue to bake for 4 minutes, or until cheese melts. Serve hot.

Cleaning Mushrooms

To clean mushrooms easily, place them in a large bowl of water. Swish the mushrooms around a few times, then lift out and drain in a colander. Remove any excess dirt with a paper towel. Since mushrooms absorb liquid quickly, do not let them soak in the water. Wash just before using to prevent discoloration.

Tomato and Basil Bruschetta

This is probably the most popular of bruschetta toppings. Although it is available at many deli counters, it is easy to make your own, especially at the peak of tomato and basil season. Tomatoes and basil are a natural combination, but you can also try other fresh herbs such as summer savory, marjoram or dill.

You can use two small regular or yellow tomatoes instead of the plum tomatoes.

MAKES 6 BRUSCHETTA

Make Ahead

Topping can be prepared up to 4 hours ahead and left at room temperature.

3	medium plum tomatoes, seeded and diced	3
1 tsp	balsamic vinegar	5 mL
2 tbsp	grated Parmesan cheese	25 mL
1 tbsp	shredded fresh basil leaves	15 mL
¼ tsp	salt	1 mL
¼ tsp	black pepper	1 mL
6	slices baguette (about ½ inch/ 1 cm thick)	6

1. In a bowl, toss together diced tomatoes, vinegar, cheese, basil, salt and pepper.
2. Arrange baguette slices on oven pan. Place under preheated broiler and broil for 1 minute per side, or until starting to color.
3. Top each bread slice with tomato mixture. Serve immediately.

> **Shredding Fresh Basil**
>
> To shred fresh basil leaves, stack 4 or 5 leaves and roll them up tightly. Slice finely using a sharp knife.

Baked Brie with Peach Cranberry Topping

A creamy, oozing spread that can be served for brunch, afternoon tea, as an appetizer or dessert. Let your imagination be the guide for the toppings. Try hot pepper jelly, mango chutney, mango salsa (page 54), cranapple sauce (page 107), green sauce (page 92) or your favorite jam or jelly. Serve with crackers, breads, raw vegetables or fruit.

MAKES 4 TO 8 SERVINGS

Variations

Pecan and Brown Sugar Topping

In a small bowl, combine ½ cup (125 mL) packed brown sugar, ¼ cup (50 mL) chopped pecans and 1 tsp (5 mL) grated lemon zest. Spoon over Brie and bake for 10 to 12 minutes, or until cheese has softened.

Fig and Port Topping

In a medium saucepan, combine 1 cup (250 mL) chopped dried figs, ½ cup (125 mL) orange juice and ½ cup (125 mL) Port. Bring to a boil and boil for 4 minutes. Remove from heat and let stand for 20 minutes. Spoon over Brie and bake for 10 to 12 minutes, or until cheese has softened. Serve with crackers and fresh cracked walnuts.

1	7-oz (200 g) round Brie cheese	1
Peach Cranberry Topping		
⅓ cup	peach or apricot jam	75 mL
⅓ cup	cranberry sauce	75 mL
2 tbsp	toasted pine nuts	25 mL

1. Place Brie on parchment-lined oven pan (make sure paper does not hang over edges of pan).

2. In a bowl, combine peach jam, cranberry sauce and pine nuts. Spoon over Brie.

3. Bake in preheated 350°F (180°C) toaster oven for 10 to 12 minutes, or until cheese has softened.

> **Toasting Pine Nuts**
>
> To toast pine nuts, spread on oven pan and bake in preheated 300°F (150°C) toaster oven for 6 minutes, or until nuts are just starting to turn golden. Store in refrigerator or freezer.

Salsa, Crab and Cheese Spread

For a lighter version of this spread, use light cream cheese, and for a very rich and creamy version, use chèvre (goat cheese). You can also use ¾ cup (175 mL) diced cooked chicken or turkey or 1 cup (250 mL) drained and rinsed cooked black beans in place of the crab. Serve in the baking dish with a small spoon for spreading on tortilla chips and fresh vegetables. Leftovers make a good sandwich filling.

MAKES 6 TO 8 SERVINGS

Make Ahead

The spread can be assembled, covered and refrigerated up to 8 hours before baking.

1	8-oz (250 g) package cream cheese, softened	1
1	6-oz (170 g) can crabmeat or tuna, drained and broken up	1
1 cup	tomato salsa	250 mL
1 cup	grated Cheddar cheese	250 mL
2 tbsp	chopped fresh parsley or cilantro	25 mL

1. Spread cheese over bottom of a shallow 8-inch (20 cm) round or square ovenproof serving dish. Top with crabmeat. Spread with salsa and sprinkle with Cheddar.

2. Bake in preheated 325°F (160°C) toaster oven for 15 to 18 minutes, or until cheese melts and spread is hot.

3. Sprinkle with parsley. Let stand for 10 minutes before serving.

Roasted Almonds

Fortunately, my cousin arrived shortly after I made these, so I sent them home with her; otherwise I would have eaten them all!

These almonds make handy hostess gifts year round, as well as a quick, easy appetizer. Store them in an airtight container in a cool place for up to one week.

Use pecans, walnuts or cashews instead of the almonds if you wish.

MAKES 1½ CUPS (375 ML)

2 tsp	olive oil	10 mL
2 tsp	pure maple syrup or packed brown sugar	10 mL
1 tsp	Worcestershire sauce	5 mL
1 tsp	coarse salt	5 mL
½ tsp	paprika (preferably smoked)	2 mL
½ tsp	dried rosemary or savory leaves	2 mL
1½ cups	unblanched or blanched almonds (about 8 oz/250 g)	375 mL

1. In a bowl, combine oil, maple syrup, Worcestershire, salt, paprika, rosemary and almonds.

2. Spread almonds over lightly greased oven pan. Bake in preheated 350°F (180°C) toaster oven for 15 to 18 minutes, or until lightly toasted. Stir two or three times during baking. Serve almonds warm or cool to room temperature. (Stir occasionally while nuts are cooling to prevent sticking.)

Smoked Paprika

This smoky spice is mainly produced in Spain. Look for it in food shops featuring Spanish or Italian specialties. It is very full-flavored, so use it sparingly at first. Store it at room temperature in a tightly covered container away from heat and humidity.

Open-face Chicken Pita

Keep frozen pitas on hand, as they defrost quickly in the toaster oven. (Bake at 250°F/120°C for 4 to 5 minutes.) Whenever you have a bit of leftover cooked chicken or turkey, make this for a quick appetizer, snack, lunch or for mid-afternoon tea.

MAKES 1 SERVING

½ cup	diced cooked chicken or turkey	125 mL
½ cup	grated Cheddar or Swiss cheese	125 mL
2 tsp	mango chutney	10 mL
1	7-inch (18 cm) pita bread	1

1. In a small bowl, combine chicken, cheese and chutney.
2. Place pita on oven pan. Spread chicken mixture over pita.
3. Bake in preheated 375°F (190°C) toaster oven for 8 to 10 minutes, or until cheese melts and pita is hot.

> **Pita Crisps**
>
> Serve these crisps with dips and spreads. Lightly brush two 7-inch (18 cm) pita breads on both sides with 2 tsp (10 mL) olive oil. Cut each pita into 12 wedges. Arrange wedges on oven pan. Bake in preheated 350°F (180°C) toaster oven for 12 to 15 minutes, or until golden and crisp. Makes 24 crisps.

Nachos

It seems that wherever there is a party or gathering of friends, there are nachos. Here is a non-traditional version.

Several kinds of tortilla chips are available, but for something different, use blue corn chips. For a more substantial dish, spoon ½ cup (125 mL) canned refried beans or canned pork and beans over the first layer of cheese. You can also top the baked nachos with shredded lettuce and chopped tomatoes and serve them with a dollop of sour cream on the side.

MAKES 3 TO 4 SERVINGS

⅓ cup	tomato pasta sauce	75 mL
1	green onion, chopped	1
2 tbsp	chopped fresh cilantro	25 mL
1 tbsp	hoisin sauce	15 mL
2 tsp	sweet Asian chili sauce	10 mL
3 cups	tortilla chips	750 mL
1¼ cups	grated Cheddar or Monterey Jack cheese	300 mL

1. In a small bowl, combine pasta sauce, green onion, cilantro, hoisin sauce and sweet Asian chili sauce.

2. Arrange half the tortilla chips on a lightly greased 9-inch (23 cm) round ovenproof serving dish (a glass pie plate works perfectly). Sprinkle with half the Cheddar and half the sauce. Arrange remaining chips over sauce. Top with remaining sauce and Cheddar.

3. Bake in preheated 400°F (200°C) toaster oven for 8 minutes, or until cheese melts.

Sweet Asian Chili Sauce

Sweet Asian chili sauce is a translucent, thickened sugar syrup containing hot pepper flakes and vinegar. It is served as a sweet/hot condiment with Thai-flavored foods such as spring rolls. It is available in supermarkets and Asian stores (the jar often has a chicken on the label).

Sacha's Snacks

My friend's young son was making these as a snack for himself and his cousins when I walked in. I asked him for the recipe and he said he just uses what is in the cupboard and fridge (provided that Mom has shopped!), but this is one version. You can mix and match various meats and cheeses, including mortadella, corned beef, mozzarella, Cheddar, etc. Try Monterey Jack cheese topped with a dab of salsa and a slice of jalapeño, sliced Brie and salami, or herbed cream cheese topped with a bit of smoked salmon or pepper jelly (bake just until the cheese melts; some cheeses will melt more quickly than others).

If there is room on the tray, Sacha sometimes makes eight at a time. Otherwise he just keeps making six until everyone is full. A chef in the making?

MAKES 6 SNACKS

6	wheat crackers (about 2 inches/5 cm square)	6
6	thin slices smoked turkey or ham	6
6	thin slices Gruyère or Fontina cheese	6

1. Arrange crackers in a single layer on oven pan. Fold meat to fit on crackers. Top with cheese slices trimmed to fit.
2. Bake in preheated 350°F (180°C) toaster oven for 8 minutes, or until cheese melts.

Fish and Seafood

Baked Lemon Salmon with Mango Salsa

This is perfect for a quick weeknight meal, yet elegant enough for entertaining. Papaya or pineapple could be used in place of mango.

Serve the salmon hot or cold.

MAKES 4 SERVINGS

1 tbsp	grated lemon zest	15 mL
2 tbsp	lemon juice	25 mL
1 tbsp	olive oil	15 mL
2 tsp	Russian-style mustard	10 mL
½ tsp	black pepper	2 mL
4	salmon fillets (about 6 oz/175 g each), skin removed	4

Mango Salsa

1	ripe mango, peeled and diced	1
2	green onions, finely chopped	2
¼ cup	chopped red bell pepper	50 mL
2 tbsp	chopped fresh cilantro	25 mL
2 tbsp	lime juice	25 mL

1. In a small bowl, whisk together lemon zest, lemon juice, oil, mustard and pepper.
2. Place salmon in a single layer in an 8-inch (2 L) square baking dish. Pour marinade over fish. Marinate for 20 minutes.
3. Bake in preheated 400°F (200°C) toaster oven for 12 to 15 minutes, or until salmon is just cooked in center.
4. Meanwhile, to prepare salsa, in a bowl, combine mango, green onions, red pepper, cilantro and lime juice. Serve salsa with salmon.

Soy-glazed Salmon

The flavors here are similar to teriyaki sauce. Serve with steamed asparagus and a rice pilaf (page 145) — cook the rice pilaf and keep warm, covered, while you are cooking the salmon. A soba noodle salad also makes a tasty accompaniment.

MAKES 4 SERVINGS

Variation

Honey Mustard Salmon
In a small bowl, combine 2 tbsp (25 mL) honey, 2 tbsp (25 mL) lemon juice, 1 tbsp (15 mL) Dijon mustard and 1 tbsp (15 mL) olive oil. Spoon over salmon in place of soy glaze.

Toasting Sesame Seeds

To toast sesame seeds, place in a small baking dish or pan. Bake in preheated 300°F (150°C) toaster oven for 6 to 8 minutes, or until golden. Stir occasionally during baking. Store extra toasted seeds in a jar in the refrigerator or freezer.

2 tbsp	packed brown sugar	25 mL
2 tbsp	soy sauce	25 mL
2 tbsp	rice vinegar or lemon juice	25 mL
1 tbsp	vegetable oil	15 mL
4	salmon fillets (about 6 oz/175 g each), skin removed	4

1. In a small bowl or measuring cup, combine brown sugar, soy sauce, vinegar and oil. Stir to dissolve sugar.
2. Arrange salmon fillets in a single layer in a lightly greased 8-inch (2 L) square baking dish. Spoon sauce over salmon.
3. Bake in preheated 400°F (200°C) toaster oven for 12 to 15 minutes, or until salmon is just cooked in center. Spoon glaze over salmon before serving.

Soba Noodle Salad

Soba noodles are made with buckwheat and wheat flour. They have a nutty flavor and go well with fish and chicken dishes. Look for them in health food stores and Asian stores. Serve them in dashi (a broth made with seaweed and soy sauce) or in this salad.

Bring a large pot of water to a boil. Add 4 oz (125 g) uncooked soba noodles and cook for 5 to 7 minutes, or until tender (do not overcook or noodles will be mushy). Drain and rinse well with cold water. Drain again.

Meanwhile, in a large bowl, combine 1/4 cup (50 mL) orange juice, 2 tbsp (25 mL) rice vinegar, 2 tbsp (25 mL) soy sauce, 2 tsp (10 mL) honey and 2 tsp (10 mL) roasted sesame oil. Add cooked noodles, 4 chopped green onions, 1 cup (250 mL) grated carrot and 1 cup (250 mL) diced cucumber. Toss thoroughly. Sprinkle with 1 tbsp (15 mL) toasted sesame seeds (see sidebar). Let stand for 30 minutes before serving. Makes 4 small servings.

Salmon in Phyllo

Each year our Rotary Club hosts a fundraising dinner and auction for 350 guests. With the help of a large group of volunteers, my friends Glen and Gord and I prepare a special four-course dinner. This is a version of a fish course we served, and it was a great hit.

Salmon fillets are usually sold in 6-oz (175 g) pieces. Cut them in half for this recipe. Arctic char can also be used.

The easiest way to cut a carrot into matchstick pieces (julienne) is to cut it in thin diagonal slices. Stack three or four slices and cut into matchstick-sized pieces.

MAKES 2 TO 4 SERVINGS

Make Ahead

Phyllo packages can be assembled, covered and refrigerated up to 6 hours before baking.

2 tbsp	butter	25 mL
1	leek, white part only, cut in matchstick pieces	1
1	carrot, cut in matchstick pieces	1
2 tbsp	chopped fresh dillweed	25 mL
2 tbsp	chopped fresh parsley	25 mL
1/4 tsp	salt	1 mL
1/4 tsp	black pepper	1 mL
4	sheets phyllo pastry, defrosted	4
1/4 cup	butter, melted	50 mL
2	salmon fillets (about 6 oz/175 g each), skin removed	2

1. In a small skillet, melt butter over medium heat. Add leek and carrot. Cook, stirring often, for 4 minutes, or until tender. Remove from heat. Stir in dill, parsley, salt and pepper. Cool.

2. To assemble, lay a sheet of phyllo pastry on counter with narrow side facing you. Brush lightly with melted butter.

3. Place one-quarter of leek mixture in center at bottom of phyllo.

4. Cut each salmon fillet in half lengthwise. Place one piece over leek mixture.

5. Fold up phyllo from bottom to cover salmon. Fold in long sides. Roll up pastry to form a cigar shape.

6. Place pastry, seam side down, on lightly greased oven pan. Brush lightly with butter. Repeat with remaining ingredients to make 4 rolls.

7. Bake in preheated 375°F (190°C) toaster oven for 25 minutes, or until golden.

Lemon Dill Tilapia

Tilapia is a mild and delicate fish similar to snapper. Haddock, sole or snapper can also be used in this recipe. The fillets should be about $\frac{1}{2}$ inch (1 cm) thick; otherwise adjust the cooking time. (Check the oven manufacturer's manual to see whether the door should be left ajar during broiling.) Serve with baby new potatoes and a green vegetable.

MAKES 2 SERVINGS

2	tilapia fillets (about 12 oz/375 g total)	2
2 tbsp	lemon juice	25 mL
1 tbsp	olive oil	15 mL
2 tbsp	chopped fresh dillweed	25 mL
$\frac{1}{4}$ tsp	salt	1 mL

1. Place fillets in a shallow baking dish. Sprinkle fish with lemon juice, oil, dill and salt. Turn fish to coat all sides. Marinate for 10 minutes.
2. Place fillets on lightly greased broiler rack placed over oven pan.
3. Broil under preheated toaster oven broiler for 10 minutes, or until fish flakes easily when tested with a fork.

Halibut Provençal

Fish retains both flavor and moistness when topped with this sauce and cooked quickly under the toaster oven broiler (check the manufacturer's manual to see whether the oven door should be left ajar when broiling). Serve it with rice or couscous.

MAKES 4 SERVINGS

Tomato Orange Sauce

2 tbsp	olive oil	25 mL
1	small onion, chopped	1
2	cloves garlic, finely chopped	2
1 cup	chopped tomato	250 mL
½ cup	dry white wine	125 mL
1 tsp	grated orange zest	5 mL
½ tsp	dried thyme leaves	2 mL
½ tsp	salt	2 mL
½ tsp	black pepper	2 mL

Fish

1 tbsp	olive oil	15 mL
1 tbsp	lemon juice	15 mL
¼ tsp	salt	1 mL
¼ tsp	black pepper	1 mL
1½ lbs	halibut fillets (4 pieces about 1 inch/2.5 cm thick)	750 g
⅓ cup	pitted black olives	75 mL
2 tsp	drained capers	10 mL
2 tbsp	chopped fresh basil or parsley	25 mL

1. To make sauce, in a medium skillet, heat olive oil over medium-high heat. Add onion and garlic. Cook, stirring occasionally, for 3 minutes, or until softened.

2. Add tomato, wine, orange zest, thyme, salt and pepper to skillet. Bring to a boil, reduce heat and simmer for 8 minutes.

3. Meanwhile, to prepare fish, in a shallow dish, combine olive oil, lemon juice, salt and pepper. Dip fish into marinade and place on lightly greased broiler rack placed over oven pan.

4. Place oven pan under preheated toaster oven broiler. Broil for 6 to 8 minutes per side, or until fish flakes lightly when tested with a fork (timing will depend on thickness of fish).

5. Place fish on a serving platter. Spoon sauce over fish and top with olives, capers and basil.

Carrot Couscous

In a medium saucepan, heat 1 tbsp (15 mL) olive oil over medium-high heat. Add 1 chopped onion and 1 cup (250 mL) grated carrot. Cook for 4 minutes, stirring occasionally, until softened.

Add $1\frac{1}{2}$ cups (375 mL) carrot juice or water and bring to a boil. Remove from heat.

Stir in 1 cup (250 mL) dried couscous, $\frac{1}{2}$ tsp (2 mL) salt and $\frac{1}{4}$ tsp (1 mL) black pepper. Cover and let stand for 10 minutes.

Stir in 2 tbsp (25 mL) chopped fresh cilantro or parsley and fluff couscous with a fork. Makes 4 servings.

Fish Fillets on Spinach Leaves

When my garden starts to produce spinach, I add it to almost everything I make, including this recipe. Swiss chard makes a good substitute. Serve with cooked rice or mashed potatoes (page 93).

MAKES 3 SERVINGS

Make Ahead

Dish can be assembled, covered and refrigerated up to 4 hours before baking.

8	large fresh spinach leaves	8
3	fish fillets, such as snapper, tilapia or salmon (about 6 oz/175 g each)	3
2	green onions, chopped	2
2 tbsp	chopped oil-packed sun-dried tomatoes	25 mL
1 tbsp	chopped fresh dillweed	15 mL
2 tbsp	dry white wine or water	25 mL
1 tbsp	olive oil	15 mL
1 tbsp	lemon juice	15 mL
¼ tsp	salt	1 mL
¼ tsp	black pepper	1 mL

1. Remove coarse stems from spinach and shred leaves. Place shredded spinach in bottom of an 8-inch (2 L) square baking dish. Arrange fish fillets over spinach, slightly overlapping if necessary.

2. Sprinkle fish with green onions, sun-dried tomatoes, dill, wine, olive oil, lemon juice, salt and pepper.

3. Cover dish tightly with foil. Bake in preheated 375°F (190°C) toaster oven for 20 to 25 minutes, or until fish flakes when tested with a fork.

Fish Fillets in Sweet and Sour Tomato Sauce

For a spicier dish, add ½ tsp (2 mL) hot pepper sauce after the sauce thickens. Crusty bread will help to mop up any juices. Serve hot or at room temperature as part of a buffet or a Mediterranean-themed meal.

MAKES 3 SERVINGS

Make Ahead

Sauce can be prepared, covered and refrigerated for up to 2 days.

2 tbsp	olive oil	25 mL
1	onion, chopped	1
2	cloves garlic, finely chopped	2
2	stalks celery, chopped	2
1	red bell pepper, seeded and diced	1
1	28-oz (796 mL) can plum tomatoes, chopped, with juices	1
¼ cup	packed brown sugar	50 mL
¼ cup	white vinegar or cider vinegar	50 mL
½ tsp	salt	2 mL
¼ tsp	black pepper	1 mL
1 lb	fish fillets (e.g., cod, haddock or halibut), cut in 4 pieces	500 g

1. In a large saucepan, heat oil over medium-high heat. Add onion, garlic, celery and red pepper. Cook for 6 minutes, or until softened, stirring often.

2. Add tomatoes, brown sugar and vinegar to saucepan. Bring to a boil. Cook, uncovered, at medium boil, stirring frequently, until sauce thickens, about 15 minutes. Sauce should be quite thick (like chili sauce), as fish will give off liquid. Reduce heat gradually as sauce thickens. Season with salt and pepper.

3. Place half of sauce in an 8-inch (2 L) square baking dish. Arrange fillets over sauce. Spoon remaining sauce over fish.

4. Bake in preheated 400°F (200°C) toaster oven for 15 to 18 minutes, or until fish is opaque and flakes when tested with a fork.

Baked Cajun Catfish

Cajun flavors are found in many dishes, from crawfish, chicken and ribs to potatoes and dressings. They are often served with beer to cool the heat.

These fillets can also be cooled slightly and served in a sandwich with mayonnaise, tomato slices and lettuce.

MAKES 2 SERVINGS

½ tsp	chili powder	2 mL
½ tsp	garlic powder	2 mL
¼ tsp	dried oregano leaves	1 mL
¼ tsp	dried thyme leaves	1 mL
¼ tsp	paprika	1 mL
¼ tsp	salt	1 mL
¼ tsp	black pepper	1 mL
Pinch	cayenne pepper	Pinch
2	catfish fillets (about 12 oz/375 g total)	2
1 tbsp	olive oil	15 mL
1 tbsp	lime juice or lemon juice	15 mL

1. In a small bowl, combine chili powder, garlic powder, oregano, thyme, paprika, salt, black pepper and cayenne.
2. Place fillets in a shallow dish. Sprinkle fish with oil and lime juice.
3. Rub seasoning mix over fish to coat all sides.
4. Place fillets in a single layer on lightly greased broiler rack placed over oven pan. Bake in preheated 400°F (200°C) toaster oven for 12 to 14 minutes, or until fish is opaque and flakes easily when tested with a fork.

Orange Pesto Fish Kabobs

Select a firm-fleshed fish such as salmon, halibut or monkfish when making kabobs. With colorful additions of red pepper and zucchini, these kabobs are an attractive addition to any menu. Serve them warm on a salad of baby greens.

MAKES 4 SERVINGS

Make Ahead

Kabobs can be assembled, covered and refrigerated up to 6 hours before broiling.

1 lb	fish fillets, cut in 1-inch (2.5 cm) chunks (about 16 chunks)	500 g
1 tbsp	basil pesto	15 mL
1 tbsp	orange juice concentrate	15 mL
½	red bell pepper, seeded and cut in 1-inch (2.5 cm) pieces	½
1	small zucchini, cut in ½-inch (1 cm) slices	1

1. In a medium bowl, combine fish chunks, pesto and orange juice concentrate. Toss to coat.
2. Thread fish, pepper and zucchini pieces onto four 6- to 8-inch (15 to 20 cm) skewers.
3. Place skewers (with exposed skewer ends near oven door to prevent burning) on lightly greased broiler rack placed over oven pan. Broil under preheated broiler for 10 to 12 minutes, or until fish flakes easily when tested with a fork. Turn once during broiling. (Check oven manual to see whether oven door should be left ajar during broiling.)

Pesto

In a food processor, combine 1 cup (250 mL) packed fresh basil leaves, ¼ cup (50 mL) toasted pine nuts, 2 peeled cloves garlic, ¼ tsp (1 mL) salt and ¼ tsp (1 mL) black pepper. Pulse until finely chopped. With machine running, pour ⅓ cup (75 mL) olive oil through feed tube. Blend in ⅓ cup (75 L) grated Parmesan cheese, scraping down sides of food processor. Makes about 1 cup (250 mL).

Refrigerate pesto for up to 4 days or freeze for up to 6 weeks. To freeze, spoon pesto in 2 tbsp (25 mL) portions on waxed paper-lined baking sheet. Freeze, then transfer to resealable plastic bags.

Roasted Fish Fillets with Crumb Topping

A simple topping of breadcrumbs adds a bit of crunch to these fillets. Try using salmon, halibut or grouper, and buy fillets that are at least 1 inch (2.5 cm) thick. Serve with ratatouille (page 138) or tartar sauce (page 69).

MAKES 4 SERVINGS

¾ cup	fresh breadcrumbs	175 mL
2 tbsp	chopped fresh basil, dillweed or parsley	25 mL
1 tbsp	olive oil	15 mL
1	clove garlic, minced	1
1 tsp	grated lemon zest	5 mL
4	fish fillets (about 6 oz/175 g each)	4
4	lemon wedges	4

1. In a small bowl, combine breadcrumbs, basil, oil, garlic and lemon zest.
2. Place fillets in a single layer on lightly greased oven pan. Press crumb mixture over top of fillets.
3. Bake in preheated 425°F (220°C) toaster oven for 12 to 15 minutes, or until fish is opaque and flakes easily when tested with a fork. Serve garnished with lemon wedges.

Salsas

Salsas are colorful, flavorful, low-fat condiments. They can be pounded, pureed or chopped; cooked or raw. Let your own whims and the seasons be your guide and invent your own house salsa (the Spanish word for sauce), or try a few of the following recipes.

Combine the ingredients and try to serve within one or two hours (they can become watery if allowed to sit too long).

- **Avocado Corn Salsa**: In a bowl, combine 1 diced ripe avocado, 1 cup (250 mL) corn kernels, $\frac{1}{2}$ cup (125 mL) diced sweet onion, 2 tbsp (25 mL) rice vinegar, 1 tsp (5 mL) chopped fresh dill or cilantro, $\frac{1}{2}$ tsp (2 mL) granulated sugar, $\frac{1}{2}$ tsp (2 mL) salt, $\frac{1}{2}$ tsp (2 mL) black pepper and a pinch hot red pepper flakes. Serve within an hour to prevent avocado from turning brown. Makes about 2 cups (500 mL).

- **Mediterranean Salsa:** In a bowl, combine 3 diced tomatoes, $\frac{1}{2}$ cup (125 mL) chopped green or black olives, 2 minced cloves garlic, 2 tbsp (25 mL) balsamic vinegar, 1 tbsp (15 mL) olive oil, 2 tbsp (25 mL) shredded fresh basil, $\frac{1}{4}$ tsp (1 mL) salt and $\frac{1}{4}$ tsp (1 mL) black pepper. Makes about 2 cups (500 mL).

- **Pineapple Salsa:** In a bowl, combine 1 cup (250 mL) diced fresh pineapple, 1 cup (250 mL) diced cucumber, 1 chopped green onion, 2 tbsp (25 mL) lemon juice, 2 tbsp (25 mL) chopped fresh cilantro or parsley and 1 tsp (5 mL) roasted sesame oil. Makes about 2 cups (500 mL).

- **Fresh Strawberry Salsa:** Spoon this salsa over baked Brie (page 47) just before serving. In a medium bowl, combine 1 cup (250 mL) coarsely chopped fresh strawberries, 1 chopped green onion, 2 tsp (10 mL) chopped jalapeño pepper, 1 tbsp (15 mL) olive oil and 1 tbsp (15 mL) orange juice. Makes about $1\frac{1}{4}$ cups (300 mL).

- **Strawberry Grape Salsa:** In a bowl, combine 1 cup (250 mL) sliced fresh strawberries, 1 cup (250 mL) halved green grapes, 2 tbsp (25 mL) chopped fresh chives, 2 tbsp (25 mL) chopped fresh mint, 1 tbsp (15 mL) rice vinegar or cider vinegar, 1 tsp (5 mL) honey and $\frac{1}{4}$ tsp (1 mL) black pepper. Makes about 2 cups (500 mL).

Pizza-flavored Fish Sticks

Frozen fish sticks are a secret comfort food for many grownups, even though most won't admit it. And, of course, kids love them, too. They are perfect for the toaster oven. Use any leftover fish sticks in sandwiches; serve in rolls or buns with mayonnaise or tartar sauce (page 69) and shredded lettuce.

MAKES 4 TO 5 SERVINGS

Variations

Cheddar and Dijon Fish Sticks

In a small bowl, combine ⅓ cup (75 mL) mayonnaise, ½ cup (125 mL) grated Cheddar cheese and 2 tsp (10 mL) Russian-style mustard. Top each fish stick with sauce during last 4 minutes of baking.

Mediterranean Fish Sticks

In a bowl, combine a 6-oz (170 mL) jar drained and chopped marinated artichoke hearts, 1 chopped tomato, 2 tbsp (25 mL) chopped black olives and 2 tbsp (25 mL) chopped fresh basil leaves. Serve alongside fish or spoon over cooked fish sticks.

12 to 14	frozen fish sticks (1 package)	12 to 14
½ cup	tomato pasta sauce	125 mL
½ cup	grated mozzarella cheese	125 mL
2 tbsp	grated Parmesan cheese	25 mL

1. Arrange fish sticks in a single layer on oven pan. Bake in preheated 425°F (220°C) toaster oven for 8 minutes per side, or until crisp.

2. Meanwhile, in a small bowl, combine pasta sauce, mozzarella and Parmesan.

3. Top each fish stick with sauce during the last 4 minutes of baking.

Salmon and Tuna Loaf

This fish loaf can be assembled quickly, and it is a favorite picnic or luncheon dish. Serve it hot with rice or new potatoes or cold with a potato salad and sliced field tomatoes. It is an easy traveler — just keep it very cold until serving time.

You can also use all salmon or all tuna.

To crush crackers easily, place in a plastic bag and crush with a rolling pin.

MAKES 4 TO 5 SERVINGS

1	7½-oz (213 g) can salmon, drained	1
1	6-oz (170 g) can water-packed tuna, drained	1
2	eggs, beaten	2
¾ cup	milk	175 mL
½ cup	cracker crumbs	125 mL
⅓ cup	finely chopped celery	75 mL
⅓ cup	finely chopped green onion	75 mL
3 tbsp	lemon juice	45 mL
2 tbsp	chopped fresh dillweed	25 mL
1 tsp	Dijon mustard	5 mL
¼ tsp	salt	1 mL
¼ tsp	black pepper	1 mL

1. In a large bowl, combine salmon and tuna and mash well.

2. Add eggs, milk, cracker crumbs, celery, green onion, lemon juice, dill, mustard, salt and pepper. Mix thoroughly.

3. Spoon mixture into a parchment-lined or greased 8- by 4-inch (1.5 L) loaf pan.

4. Bake in preheated 350°F (180°C) toaster oven for 50 minutes, or until center is firm and top is golden. If you are serving salmon cold, let rest in pan for 25 minutes before removing (loosen edges with a knife). To serve hot, let stand for 5 minutes before turning out of loaf pan.

Salmon and Potato Scallop

In our family, this last-minute dish was the answer on wash day or gardening day, when the clock moved too quickly. Serve it with fresh shelled peas, sugar snap peas or green beans. Include this on brunch or lunch menus, too. For the best color, use red sockeye salmon.

Use potatoes that bake well, such as Yukon Gold or baking potatoes. Avoid new potatoes, since they do not absorb moisture well.

MAKES 4 SERVINGS

1	7½-oz (213 g) can red sockeye salmon	1
1	onion, thinly sliced	1
1	stalk celery, chopped	1
3	potatoes (about 1½ lbs/750 g total), peeled and thinly sliced	3
½ tsp	salt	2 mL
½ tsp	black pepper	2 mL
2	eggs	2
1¼ cups	milk	300 mL
½ cup	fresh breadcrumbs	125 mL
2 tbsp	butter, melted	25 mL
2 tbsp	chopped fresh parsley	25 mL

1. Drain juices from salmon. Spread salmon over bottom of a lightly greased 8-inch (2 L) square baking dish. Top with onion and celery. Arrange potato slices over top. Sprinkle with salt and pepper.
2. In a bowl, whisk together eggs and milk. Pour over potatoes.
3. In a separate bowl, combine breadcrumbs, melted butter and parsley. Sprinkle over potatoes.
4. Bake in preheated 350°F (180°C) toaster oven for 50 minutes, or until potatoes are tender.

Herbed Crumbed Scallops

This technique for breading the scallops can also be used with thin pieces of chicken, fish and even eggplant slices. Serve as an appetizer or main course.

MAKES 3 TO 4 SERVINGS

Make Ahead

If scallops are well dried, they can be breaded up to 3 hours ahead of time and refrigerated, uncovered, until baking.

16	large scallops (about 1 lb/500 g total)	16
1/4 cup	all-purpose flour	50 mL
2	eggs	2
1 1/2 cups	fresh breadcrumbs	375 mL
1/4 cup	chopped mixed fresh herbs, e.g., parsley, dillweed and tarragon	50 mL

Tartar Sauce

1/2 cup	mayonnaise	125 mL
3 tbsp	chopped dill or sweet pickle	45 mL
1 tbsp	chopped fresh dillweed	15 mL
1/2 tsp	prepared horseradish	2 mL
1/4 tsp	salt	1 mL
1/4 tsp	black pepper	1 mL

1. Pat scallops dry. Place flour in a shallow dish. Beat eggs in a second shallow dish. In a third shallow dish, mix together breadcrumbs and herbs.

2. Dust scallops with flour. Roll in egg mixture and then in breadcrumbs, turning to coat all sides. Arrange in a single layer on lightly greased broiler rack set over oven pan.

3. Bake in preheated 400°F (200°C) toaster oven for 15 minutes, or until scallops are opaque and crumbs are golden and crisp.

4. Meanwhile, to prepare sauce, in a small bowl, combine mayonnaise, pickle, dill, horseradish, salt and pepper. Serve with scallops.

Seafood Rice Gratin

The rich flavors of seafood and sauce combine to make this excellent special-occasion dish. It can also be served as a starter before a light main course, or on a brunch or luncheon buffet. Using real crab or lobster will make this even more enticing. Serve it with a salad of baby greens.

MAKES 4 SERVINGS

Make Ahead

Prepare sauce up to the end of Step 3. Cover and refrigerate until cold. Combine with seafood. Assemble dish, cover and refrigerate up to 6 hours before baking.

2 tbsp	butter	25 mL
1	onion, chopped	1
1	stalk celery, finely chopped	1
½ cup	chopped red bell pepper	125 mL
2 tbsp	all-purpose flour	25 mL
1½ cups	milk	375 mL
1 cup	grated Swiss cheese	250 mL
1 tbsp	chopped fresh dillweed	15 mL
1 tsp	chopped fresh tarragon, or ¼ tsp (1 mL) dried	5 mL
½ tsp	salt	2 mL
¼ tsp	black pepper	1 mL
¼ tsp	hot red pepper sauce	1 mL
8 oz	chopped imitation crab	250 g
8 oz	diced shrimp or scallops, patted dry	250 g
1½ cups	cooked white rice	375 mL
½ cup	fresh breadcrumbs	125 mL
2 tbsp	grated Parmesan cheese	25 mL

1. In a large saucepan, melt butter over medium heat. Add onion, celery and red pepper. Cook, stirring occasionally, for 4 minutes, or until softened.
2. Stir in flour. Cook, stirring, for 2 minutes without browning. Whisk in milk. Cook, stirring, for 5 minutes, or until sauce thickens. Remove from heat.
3. Stir in Swiss cheese, dill, tarragon, salt, pepper and hot pepper sauce.
4. Stir in crab and shrimp.
5. Spoon rice into bottom of a lightly greased 6-cup (1.5 L) baking dish. Spoon seafood mixture over rice. Sprinkle top with breadcrumbs and Parmesan.
6. Bake in preheated 375°F (190°C) toaster oven for 30 to 35 minutes, or until top is golden and sauce is bubbling.

Poultry

Roast Chicken with Orange and Sage

A small chicken roasts to a beautiful golden brown in the toaster oven, and it is easy to prepare. Garnish with fresh orange sections and serve with rice or mashed potatoes (page 93), or chill thoroughly and serve with potato salad.

MAKES 4 TO 5 SERVINGS

1	3-lb (1.5 kg) chicken	1
½ tsp	salt	2 mL
½ tsp	black pepper	2 mL
½	orange, cut in sections	½
4	cloves garlic, peeled and halved	4
3	sprigs fresh sage, or 1 tsp (5 mL) dried	3

1. Pat chicken dry and sprinkle cavity with half the salt and pepper. Place orange sections, garlic and sage in cavity. Tuck chicken wing tips under back and tie legs together. Place breast side up on broiler rack set over oven pan. Sprinkle with remaining salt and pepper.

2. Roast in preheated 350°F (180°C) toaster oven for 1 hour and 20 minutes, or until juices run clear or a meat thermometer registers 180°F (82°C) when inserted into inner thigh.

3. Remove chicken from oven and cover loosely with foil. Let stand for 15 minutes before carving.

Chicken Drumsticks with Barbecue Sauce

Take advantage of specials on large quantities of drumsticks and freeze extra in smaller quantities for future meals.

Serve these finger-lickin' good drumsticks with garlic bread (page 168), baked potatoes (page 130) or stir-fried rice (page 110) and a salad. For a finishing golden-brown touch, place the drumsticks under the toaster oven broiler for a minute or two just before serving.

MAKES 3 SERVINGS

¾ cup	homemade or storebought barbecue sauce	175 mL
2 tbsp	red wine vinegar or balsamic vinegar	25 mL
1 tsp	Dijon mustard	5 mL
1 tsp	prepared horseradish	5 mL
6	skinless chicken drumsticks or thighs	6

1. In a small bowl, combine barbecue sauce, vinegar, mustard and horseradish.
2. Arrange drumsticks in a single layer in a lightly greased 8-inch (2 L) baking dish. Spoon sauce over and turn chicken to coat.
3. Bake in preheated 375°F (190°C) toaster oven for 45 to 50 minutes, or until juices run clear. Turn drumsticks halfway through cooking time. Baste 3 or 4 times during cooking.

Barbecue Sauce

In a large saucepan, heat 2 tbsp (25 mL) olive oil over medium-high heat. Add 2 finely chopped onions and 6 finely chopped cloves garlic. Cook for 4 minutes until softened.

Add 1½ cups (375 mL) tomato sauce, ¾ cup (175 mL) water, ⅓ cup (75 mL) cider vinegar, ⅓ cup (75 mL) hoisin sauce, ¼ cup (50 mL) honey, 2 tbsp (25 mL) Worcestershire sauce, 2 tbsp (25 mL) Dijon mustard, 1 tsp (5 mL) ground cumin and 1 tsp (5 mL) dried oregano leaves. Simmer, stirring occasionally, for 30 to 35 minutes, or until thickened. Sauce can be refrigerated for three days or frozen for six weeks. Makes about 3½ cups (875 mL).

Tandoori Chicken with Raita

This is a very relaxed version of chicken tandoori, which is traditionally cooked in a hot tandoor oven. The yogurt-and-spice marinade tenderizes and flavors the chicken.

Serve with green beans and raita, a refreshing yogurt salad that is often served with spicy dishes. (It can also be served as a spread or dip.)

MAKES 4 SERVINGS

Tandoori Chicken

½ cup	unflavored yogurt	125 mL
2	cloves garlic, minced	2
2 tsp	chopped gingerroot	10 mL
2 tbsp	lemon juice	25 mL
½ tsp	paprika	2 mL
½ tsp	ground cumin	2 mL
½ tsp	ground coriander	2 mL
¼ tsp	ground cardamom or cinnamon	1 mL
¼ tsp	cayenne pepper	1 mL
4	boneless, skinless chicken breasts (about 6 oz/175 g each)	4

Raita

½	English cucumber, grated	½
½ tsp	salt	2 mL
¾ cup	unflavored yogurt	175 mL
½ cup	grated carrot	125 mL
½ tsp	granulated sugar	2 mL
¼ tsp	ground cumin	1 mL
2 tbsp	chopped fresh chives or green onion	25 mL
2 tbsp	chopped fresh mint	25 mL

1. To prepare chicken, in a small bowl, combine yogurt, garlic, ginger, lemon juice, paprika, cumin, coriander, cardamom and cayenne.

2. Arrange chicken breasts in a single layer in an 8-inch (2 L) baking dish. Pour marinade over chicken and turn to coat. Cover and refrigerate for 6 to 24 hours.

3. Arrange chicken breasts on lightly greased broiler rack set over oven pan. Bake, uncovered, in preheated 375°F (190°C) toaster oven for 25 to 30 minutes, or until juices run clear.

4. Meanwhile, to prepare raita, combine grated cucumber with salt in a sieve placed over a bowl. Let stand for 25 minutes. Gently squeeze out excess moisture.

5. In a clean bowl, combine cucumber, yogurt, carrot, sugar, cumin, chives and mint. Serve raita with chicken.

Sautéed Green Beans

In a large skillet, heat 1 tbsp (15 mL) vegetable oil over medium-high heat. Add 1 thinly sliced onion, 1 tbsp (15 mL) finely chopped gingerroot and 2 chopped cloves garlic. Cook, stirring occasionally, for 3 minutes, or until softened and starting to color.

Add 1 lb (500 g) green beans (cut in 1-inch/2.5 cm pieces), 1 chopped tomato, $\frac{1}{4}$ cup (50 mL) water, $\frac{1}{2}$ tsp (2 mL) ground cumin and $\frac{1}{4}$ tsp (1 mL) salt. Bring to a boil. Cover and reduce heat and simmer, stirring occasionally, for 8 to 10 minutes, or until beans are tender. Makes 4 servings.

Caesar Chicken

A bottle of Caesar salad dressing is the mystery ingredient here. It adds great flavor and makes the chicken moist and tender. These chicken breasts can also be chilled, sliced and served over — what else — Caesar salad. For variety, use a different prepared creamy salad dressing, such as buttermilk, ranch, creamy dill, etc.

MAKES 4 SERVINGS

½ cup	prepared Caesar dressing	125 mL
⅓ cup	fresh breadcrumbs	75 mL
¼ cup	grated Parmesan cheese	50 mL
4	boneless, skinless chicken breasts (about 6 oz/175 g each)	4

1. Pour dressing into a shallow dish. In a separate shallow dish, combine breadcrumbs and Parmesan.
2. Dip chicken breasts in dressing, then roll in breadcrumb mixture to coat, pressing in crumbs. Arrange in a single layer on lightly greased oven pan.
3. Bake in preheated 375°F (190°C) toaster oven for 25 to 30 minutes, or until juices run clear.

Chicken Curry with Apples

This slightly spicy chicken dish has lots of juices, so serve it over steamed rice. Garnish with 2 tbsp (25 mL) chopped fresh mint, cilantro or shredded coconut if you wish.

You can also make this using ham instead of chicken, but omit the salt.

MAKES 4 SERVINGS

2 tbsp	vegetable oil, divided	25 mL
1 lb	boneless, skinless chicken breasts, cut in 1-inch (2.5 cm) pieces	500 g
1	onion, thinly sliced	1
1 tbsp	chopped gingerroot	15 mL
2	apples, peeled and cut in ½-inch (1 cm) pieces	2
2 tsp	curry powder	10 mL
1 cup	chopped fresh tomatoes	250 mL
1 cup	chicken stock	250 mL
3 tbsp	mango chutney	45 mL
½ tsp	salt	2 mL
¼ tsp	black pepper	1 mL

1. In a large skillet, heat 1 tbsp (15 mL) oil over medium-high heat. Pat chicken pieces dry and cook, stirring occasionally, until golden, about 6 minutes. Spoon into a 6-cup (1.5 L) casserole (with lid).

2. Heat remaining 1 tbsp (15 mL) oil in skillet. Add onion, ginger and apples. Cook, stirring, for 4 minutes. Add curry powder and cook for 30 seconds.

3. Stir in tomatoes, stock, chutney, salt and pepper. Bring to a boil. Pour sauce over chicken.

4. Bake, covered, in preheated 350°F (180°C) toaster oven for 35 minutes, or until mixture is bubbling and chicken juices run clear.

Chicken Cacciatore

This popular dish is also known as chicken hunter style. Serve it over buttered noodles.

MAKES 3 SERVINGS

2 tbsp	olive oil, divided	25 mL
6	boneless, skinless chicken thighs (about 1½ lbs/750 g total)	6
1	onion, thinly sliced	1
2	cloves garlic, finely chopped	2
1 cup	sliced mushrooms	250 mL
¼ cup	dry white wine or chicken stock	50 mL
1 cup	pureed canned tomatoes	250 mL
2 tbsp	tomato paste	25 mL
2 tsp	chopped fresh rosemary, or ½ tsp (2 mL) dried	10 mL
½ tsp	salt	2 mL
¼ tsp	black pepper	1 mL

1. In a large skillet, heat 1 tbsp (15 mL) oil over medium-high heat. Pat chicken thighs dry. Cook until browned on all sides, about 6 minutes. Transfer to 6-cup (1.5 L) casserole (with lid).

2. Heat remaining 1 tbsp (15 mL) oil in skillet. Add onion, garlic and mushrooms. Cook, stirring occasionally, for 4 minutes.

3. Add wine, tomatoes, tomato paste, rosemary, salt and pepper. Bring to a boil. Pour sauce over chicken.

4. Bake, covered, in preheated 375°F (190°C) toaster oven for 40 minutes, or until sauce is bubbling and chicken juices run clear.

Swedish Chicken Meatballs

This version of chicken meatballs is Stroganoff-like in flavor because of the mushroom sauce. Serve it with mashed potatoes (page 93), over rye toast or with buttered noodles. Beets tossed with fresh dill make a colorful side dish.

You can also use ground turkey in this recipe, or a combination of ground pork and veal.

MAKES 3 TO 4 SERVINGS

1 lb	ground chicken	500 g
½ cup	fresh breadcrumbs	125 mL
½ cup	finely chopped onion	125 mL
1	egg, beaten	1
1 tsp	Worcestershire sauce	5 mL
½ tsp	salt	2 mL
¼ tsp	black pepper	1 mL
¼ tsp	ground nutmeg	1 mL
Mushroom Sauce		
1	10-oz (284 mL) can condensed cream of mushroom soup, undiluted	1
¼ cup	milk or chicken stock	50 mL
2 tbsp	dry sherry or orange juice	25 mL
1 tsp	Dijon mustard	5 mL

1. In a large bowl, combine ground chicken, breadcrumbs, onion, egg, Worcestershire, salt, pepper and nutmeg. Shape into 1½-inch (7 cm) meatballs (you should have about 16). If mixture is sticky, dip hands in cold water. Place meatballs in a single layer in a lightly greased 8-inch (2 L) square baking dish.

2. In a bowl, combine soup, milk, sherry and mustard. Pour over meatballs.

3. Bake in preheated 375°F (190°C) toaster oven for 40 to 45 minutes, or until meatballs are cooked through and sauce is bubbling.

Chicken with Orange

Serve this for a special occasion. Bring out the good tablecloth and linen serviettes and light the candles. It is worth buying Port for this dish, but you could also just use additional red wine. Shop for whole chicken breasts with the wings attached and skin intact, or ask your butcher for a special order. Serve with mashed potatoes (page 93) and an arugula salad.

MAKES 4 SERVINGS

Make Ahead

Sauce can be prepared, covered and refrigerated up to 2 days ahead.

4	single chicken breasts, with skin and bone (about 8 oz/250 g each)	4
¼ tsp	salt	1 mL
¼ tsp	black pepper	1 mL
Orange Sauce		
2	oranges	2
¼ cup	granulated sugar	50 mL
¼ cup	red wine vinegar	50 mL
½ cup	chicken stock	125 mL
¼ cup	Port	50 mL
¼ cup	dry red wine	50 mL
1 tbsp	butter, softened	15 mL
1 tbsp	all-purpose flour	15 mL
2 tbsp	orange liqueur or orange juice concentrate	25 mL
4	orange slices	4

1. Remove the first two parts of chicken wings and freeze for making chicken stock. Pat chicken dry. Place on oven pan or shallow baking dish. Sprinkle with salt and pepper.

2. Bake chicken in preheated 400°F (200°C) toaster oven for 35 minutes, or until juices run clear and meat thermometer registers 170°F (75°C) when inserted into thickest part.

3. Meanwhile, to prepare sauce, peel zest from oranges with a potato peeler and cut zest into thin strips (or use a zester).

4. Bring a small pot of water to a boil. Add strips to water and cook for 45 seconds. Drain and refresh under cold water.

5. Squeeze juice from oranges and reserve juice.
6. In a medium saucepan, combine sugar and vinegar. Bring to a boil over medium-high heat and cook, stirring occasionally, until syrup is golden brown (do not burn), about 6 to 8 minutes.
7. Remove saucepan from heat and add stock slowly to prevent splattering. Return to heat, and cook, stirring, for 3 minutes to dissolve caramel. Add Port, wine and reserved orange juice. Bring to a boil and cook for 8 minutes.
8. In a small dish, knead together butter and flour. Gradually stir into sauce to thicken slightly. Remove from heat. Stir in liqueur and reserved orange strips.
9. Spoon sauce over cooked chicken breasts. Garnish with orange slices.

> ### Cooking with Lemons, Limes and Oranges
>
> If a recipe calls for citrus zest and juice, remove the zest before juicing. Wash the fruit first in soapy water and rinse well to remove any residue. Dry the fruit well and remove the zest using a potato peeler, zester or kitchen rasp. Soften the fruit by rolling it on the counter before juicing.

Chicken Breasts with Pesto and Mozzarella

For color, serve this with broccoli and mashed sweet potatoes. Slice any leftover chicken and serve cold in a sandwich or as part of a salad.

MAKES 4 SERVINGS

4	boneless, skinless chicken breasts (about 6 oz/175 g each)	4
2	cloves garlic, minced	2
2 tbsp	lemon juice	25 mL
1 tbsp	olive oil	15 mL
¼ tsp	salt	1 mL
¼ tsp	black pepper	1 mL
¼ cup	basil pesto (page 63)	50 mL
4	slices mozzarella or Fontina cheese	4

1. Arrange chicken breasts in a shallow dish in a single layer.
2. In a measuring cup or small bowl, combine garlic, lemon juice, oil, salt and pepper. Pour over chicken and turn chicken to coat. Marinate for 20 minutes.
3. Arrange chicken on lightly greased oven pan in a single layer. Bake in preheated 375°F (190°C) toaster oven for 25 minutes.
4. Spread pesto over chicken. Top with cheese slices. Return to oven and bake for 5 minutes, or until juices run clear and cheese is melted and golden.

Chicken Osso Bucco

The flavors of the traditional veal dish have been borrowed for this chicken version. It is a great dish to make ahead. Serve it with couscous (page 59), rice or noodles.

MAKES 3 SERVINGS

¼ cup	all-purpose flour	50 mL
¼ tsp	salt	1 mL
¼ tsp	black pepper	1 mL
6	boneless, skinless chicken thighs (about 1½ lbs/750 g total)	6
2 tbsp	olive oil, divided	25 mL
1	onion, chopped	1
2	carrots, chopped	2
2	stalks celery, chopped	2
2	cloves garlic, finely chopped	2
1 tsp	grated lemon zest	5 mL
1½ cups	chopped fresh or canned tomatoes	375 mL
½ cup	dry white wine	125 mL

Garnish

2 tbsp	chopped fresh parsley	25 mL
2	cloves garlic, minced	2
1 tsp	grated lemon zest	5 mL

1. Combine flour, salt and pepper in a shallow dish. Dip chicken pieces into flour mixture and coat on all sides.

2. In a large skillet, heat 1 tbsp (15 mL) olive oil over medium-high heat. Add chicken and brown on all sides, about 6 minutes. Transfer to an 8-cup (2 L) casserole (with lid).

3. Heat remaining 1 tbsp (15 mL) oil in skillet. Add onion, carrots, celery and garlic. Cook, stirring occasionally, for 6 minutes, or until softened.

4. Add lemon zest, tomatoes and wine to skillet. Bring mixture to a boil.

5. Pour sauce over chicken. Bake, covered, in preheated 375°F (190°C) toaster oven for 35 minutes, or until bubbly and chicken juices run clear.

6. Meanwhile, to prepare garnish, in a small bowl, combine parsley, minced garlic and lemon zest. Sprinkle on chicken before serving.

Citrus Chicken with Romesco Sauce

The flavors of Spain dominate in this sauce traditionally made with nuts and peppers. Couscous (page 59) or rice and green beans (page 75) will round out the meal. The sauce can also be served as a dip or spread with pita bread and fresh vegetables, or you can toss it with pasta.

MAKES 4 SERVINGS

Make Ahead

Sauce can be prepared, covered and refrigerated up to a day ahead.

Variation

Citrus Fish with Roasted Garlic Romesco Sauce
Instead of chicken, use four 6-oz (175 g) fish fillets. Marinate for only 10 minutes. Bake fish for 12 to 15 minutes, or until fish flakes easily when tested with a fork (baking time will depend on thickness of fillets). For sauce, use one head roasted garlic puree (page 85) instead of raw garlic.

4	boneless, skinless chicken breasts (about 6 oz/175 g each)	4
1 tsp	grated orange zest	5 mL
1 tsp	grated lemon zest	5 mL
2 tbsp	orange juice	25 mL
1 tbsp	lemon juice	15 mL
1 tbsp	olive oil	15 mL
½ tsp	dried tarragon leaves	2 mL
¼ tsp	salt	1 mL
¼ tsp	black pepper	1 mL

Romesco Sauce

¼ cup	blanched almonds	50 mL
1	slice Italian or French bread, broken up	1
1	clove garlic, chopped	1
1	7-oz (200 mL) jar roasted red peppers, drained, or 2 small roasted red bell peppers (page 40)	1
1	6-oz (170 mL) jar marinated artichoke hearts, drained	1
3 tbsp	olive oil	45 mL
2 tbsp	red wine vinegar	25 mL
½ tsp	paprika (preferably smoked)	2 mL

1. Flatten chicken breasts slightly by placing between sheets of parchment or waxed paper and pounding gently using a meat pounder or rolling pin until chicken is an even thickness. Place chicken in a shallow dish.

2. In a small bowl, whisk together orange zest, lemon zest, orange juice, lemon juice, oil, tarragon, salt and pepper. Pour over chicken. Turn to coat. Cover and refrigerate chicken for 30 minutes or up to 6 hours.

3. Place chicken on lightly greased broiler pan set over oven pan. Bake in preheated 375°F (190°C) toaster oven for 25 to 30 minutes, or until chicken juices run clear.

4. Meanwhile, to prepare sauce, chop almonds in food processor until coarsely chopped. Add bread and chop until fine. Add garlic, red peppers, artichokes, oil, vinegar and paprika. Process until smooth. Serve sauce over chicken.

Roasted Garlic

To roast garlic, cut tops off 4 to 6 heads to expose cloves. Pour 1 tbsp (15 mL) olive oil into a small parchment-lined baking dish. Swirl garlic in oil, cut side down, to coat surface. Bake in preheated 350°F (180°C) toaster oven for 35 to 40 minutes, or until garlic is soft when squeezed.

Wrap heads individually and refrigerate for up to three days or freeze for up to six weeks. Before using, bring garlic to room temperature and squeeze cloves from skin into a small dish. Mash roasted garlic into a puree.

Chinese Jerk Chicken Wings

Chicken wings are great snack food but can also serve as luncheon or casual dinner fare. Serve with coleslaw and sliced tomatoes. Have wet hand towels available to tidy the fingers!

MAKES 2 SERVINGS

2 lbs	chicken wings	1 kg
2	green onions, coarsely chopped	2
2	cloves garlic, peeled	2
1	jalapeño pepper, seeded and coarsely chopped	1
1 tbsp	coarsely chopped gingerroot	15 mL
¼ cup	orange juice	50 mL
2 tbsp	soy sauce	25 mL
1 tbsp	Dijon mustard	15 mL
1 tbsp	rice vinegar	15 mL
¼ tsp	hot red pepper sauce	1 mL
2 tsp	ground coriander	10 mL
¼ tsp	ground allspice	1 mL
¼ tsp	salt	1 mL
¼ tsp	black pepper	1 mL

1. Cut wing tips from wings (freeze and reserve for chicken stock). Cut remaining wings into two pieces at joint. Place in a large bowl.

2. In a food processor, combine green onions, garlic, jalapeño, ginger, orange juice, soy sauce, mustard, vinegar, hot pepper sauce, coriander, allspice, salt and pepper. Puree to form a paste.

3. Add paste to chicken wings and toss to coat. Cover and refrigerate for up to 4 hours.

4. Arrange wings on broiler rack set over oven pan. Bake in preheated 400°F (200°C) toaster oven for 15 minutes. Turn wings and cook for 15 minutes longer. To crisp wings, place under preheated toaster oven broiler for 5 minutes before serving.

Pecan-crusted Chicken

The crunch and flavor of pecans add a whole new sensation to chicken. Serve this on top of a spinach and orange salad for a lunch or light supper. For an even consistency, chop the pecans in the food processor using the pulse button. Be careful not to overprocess, or you will end up with nut butter.

MAKES 4 SERVINGS

1	egg	1
1 tbsp	vegetable oil	15 mL
1½ cups	chopped pecans	375 mL
4	boneless skinless chicken breasts, about 6 oz (175 g) each	4

1. In a shallow dish, beat together egg and oil. Place pecans in a separate shallow dish.
2. Dip chicken breasts into egg mixture, turning to coat both sides. Roll chicken in pecans, pressing in crumbs. Place in a single layer on lightly greased oven pan.
3. Bake in preheated 400°F (200°C) toaster oven for 15 minutes. Turn chicken and continue to bake for 10 to 15 minutes, or until juices run clear and chicken is brown and crispy.

Chicken Tetrazzini

This version of chicken tetrazzini uses bow-tie pasta. Of course, diced turkey could be used instead of chicken, or even cooked shrimp.

MAKES 3 OR 4 SERVINGS

1½ cups	uncooked bow-tie pasta (about 4 oz/125 g)	375 mL
2 tbsp	butter	25 mL
1	onion, chopped	1
1	clove garlic, finely chopped	1
1 cup	sliced mushrooms	250 mL
2 tbsp	all-purpose flour	25 mL
1½ cups	milk or chicken stock	375 mL
½ tsp	salt	2 mL
¼ tsp	black pepper	1 mL
Pinch	ground nutmeg	Pinch
1 cup	diced cooked chicken	250 mL
½ cup	fresh or frozen peas	125 mL
2 tbsp	grated Parmesan cheese	25 mL
2 tbsp	slivered almonds (optional)	25 mL

1. In a large saucepan, cook pasta in a large amount of boiling salted water for 8 to 10 minutes, or until just tender. Drain well. (You should have about 2¼ cups/550 mL cooked pasta.)

2. Meanwhile, melt butter in a large saucepan over medium heat. Add onion, garlic and mushrooms and cook, stirring often, for 5 minutes. Add flour and cook, stirring, for 3 minutes.

3. Stir in milk. Bring to a boil, reduce heat and simmer, stirring occasionally, for 5 minutes. Remove from heat and season with salt, pepper and nutmeg.

4. Stir in chicken, peas and drained pasta. Spoon mixture into a lightly greased 6-cup (1.5 L) baking dish. Sprinkle with Parmesan and almonds, if using.

5. Bake in preheated 350°F (180°C) toaster oven for 30 to 35 minutes, or until top is golden and mixture is bubbling.

Cornish Hens with Ginger Sesame Glaze

Roasted to a golden brown in the toaster oven, a Cornish hen will serve one to two people. Since this has an Asian flavor, stir-fried rice (page 110) would be a suitable side dish, along with steamed asparagus for color.

MAKES 2 TO 4 SERVINGS

2	Cornish hens (about 1½ lbs/750 g each)	2
¼ tsp	salt	1 mL
¼ tsp	black pepper	1 mL
2 tbsp	honey	25 mL
2 tbsp	soy sauce	25 mL
2 tbsp	lemon juice	25 mL
1 tbsp	roasted sesame oil	15 mL
½ tsp	ground ginger	2 mL

1. Sprinkle cavity of hens with salt and pepper. Tie legs together.
2. Place hens in a shallow baking dish. Bake in preheated 375°F (190°C) toaster oven for 30 minutes.
3. Meanwhile, in a small bowl, combine honey, soy sauce, lemon juice, sesame oil and ginger. Baste hens with glaze and continue to cook for 40 minutes, or until juices run clear when thigh is pierced. Spoon glaze over hens 2 or 3 times during final baking, and turn pan if necessary for more even browning.
4. Remove hens to a platter. Cover loosely with foil and let stand for 10 minutes before serving.

Turkey Breast with Maple Chipotle Glaze

Single turkey breasts are now a familiar item at the meat counter. Any leftovers can be sliced for sandwiches or a salad. Mashed potatoes (page 93) are a favorite accompaniment, along with Brussels sprouts and turnip.

MAKES 4 SERVINGS

1	single turkey breast, with skin and bone (about 2 lbs/1 kg)	1
2 tbsp	pure maple syrup	25 mL
1 tbsp	chipotle puree	15 mL
1 tbsp	Dijon mustard	15 mL

1. Place turkey breast on foil- or parchment-lined oven pan (make sure edges of foil or parchment do not extend beyond edges of pan).
2. Bake in preheated 350°F (180°C) toaster oven for 1 hour and 50 minutes, or until a meat thermometer registers 170°F (75°C) when inserted into thickest part of breast.
3. Meanwhile, in a small bowl, combine maple syrup, chipotle puree and mustard. Baste turkey 3 times during last 30 minutes of roasting, adding $\frac{1}{4}$ cup (50 mL) water to pan if glaze caramelizes too much.
4. Remove turkey to a serving platter. Cover loosely with foil and let stand for 15 minutes before carving.

Chipotle Peppers

Chipotle peppers are smoked jalapeño peppers in adobo sauce. They are much hotter than regular jalapeños and are available in cans or jars at specialty food shops and some supermarkets. When you buy a can, puree the peppers and sauce and freeze in small portions.

Meat

Striploin Steak Roast with Green Sauce

A thick striploin steak produces a small tender roast with the simplest of seasonings. Montreal steak spice is the secret ingredient. It is usually located in the spice/herb section of the supermarket, but you can also use your own favorite seasoning mix. Green sauce (also called salsa verde) is a full-flavored condiment to serve alongside the carved steak. Just add sliced tomatoes, mashed potatoes (page 93) or a pasta salad.

MAKES 3 TO 4 SERVINGS

Make Ahead

Green sauce can be prepared, covered and refrigerated up to a day ahead.

Green Sauce

½ cup	packed fresh parsley leaves	125 mL
3	green onions, coarsely chopped	3
1	slice white bread, crust removed, cut in cubes	1
1 tbsp	red wine vinegar	15 mL
1	anchovy fillet, mashed, or 1 tsp (5 mL) anchovy paste	1
2 tsp	drained capers	10 mL
¼ cup	olive oil	50 mL
¼ tsp	salt	1 mL
¼ tsp	black pepper	1 mL

Roast

2	cloves garlic, minced	2
1 tbsp	lime juice or lemon juice	15 mL
1 tbsp	Worcestershire sauce	15 mL
1 tbsp	olive oil	15 mL
1 tbsp	Montreal steak spice	15 mL
1	striploin steak (about 1 lb/500 g), 1½ inches (4 cm) thick	1

1. To prepare sauce, chop parsley and green onions in food processor. Add bread cubes, vinegar, anchovy and capers. Puree, then pour in olive oil and combine well. Season with salt and pepper.

2. To prepare roast, combine garlic, lime juice, Worcestershire and oil in a flat dish. Place steak spice in a second flat dish.

3. Trim fat from steak. Dip both sides of steak into marinade mixture. Roll steak in spice to coat. Place on broiler rack set over oven pan.

4. Bake in preheated 375°F (190°C) toaster oven for 25 to 30 minutes, or until a meat thermometer registers 140°F (60°C) for rare to medium-rare.

5. Cover steak loosely with foil. Let stand for 10 minutes before carving in thin slices. Serve with green sauce.

Mashed Potatoes with Corn

In a large saucepan, cook 2 lbs (1 kg) potatoes (peeled and cut in 2-inch/5 cm pieces) in boiling salted water for 20 minutes, or until tender. Drain well.

Meanwhile, in a medium skillet, heat 2 tbsp (25 mL) butter over medium heat. Add 1 cup (250 mL) fresh or frozen and defrosted corn kernels, 2 chopped green onions, $\frac{1}{2}$ tsp (2 mL) salt and $\frac{1}{4}$ tsp (1 mL) black pepper. Cook, stirring, for 2 minutes, or until corn is tender.

Mash potatoes well, adding $\frac{1}{2}$ cup (125 mL) milk. Stir in corn mixture. Makes 3 to 4 servings.

Oven Beef Stew

Another comfort food favorite during the chilly winter months. Stews are best when cooked slowly for a long period of time. They are easy to tend to — just stir occasionally. Since stews reheat well, this is a great dish to make ahead. Refrigerate for up to two days. Let stand at room temperature for 30 minutes, then reheat in the toaster oven, covered, at 325°F (160°C) for 40 to 45 minutes, or until hot. Serve with coleslaw and biscuits (page 170).

MAKES 3 TO 4 SERVINGS

3 tbsp	all-purpose flour	45 mL
½ tsp	salt	2 mL
½ tsp	black pepper	2 mL
2 tbsp	vegetable oil	25 mL
12 oz	lean stewing beef, cut in 1-inch (2.5 cm) pieces	375 g
1 cup	beef stock	250 mL
2 tbsp	tomato paste	25 mL
1 tbsp	Worcestershire sauce	15 mL
1	onion, cut in large pieces	1
2	cloves garlic, finely chopped	2
1	stalk celery, sliced	1
1	large potato, peeled and cut in ¾-inch (2 cm) pieces	1
2	carrots, peeled and cut in ½-inch (1 cm) pieces	2
1 cup	quartered mushrooms	250 mL
½ cup	fresh or frozen peas	125 mL

1. In a shallow dish, combine flour, salt and pepper. Coat beef pieces with seasoned flour.

2. Heat oil in a large skillet over medium-high heat. Brown beef on all sides, about 8 minutes. Transfer to an 8-cup (2 L) casserole (with lid).

3. Sprinkle any remaining seasoned flour into skillet. Add stock, tomato paste and Worcestershire. Bring to a boil, stirring to deglaze pan.

4. Add onion, garlic, celery, potato, carrots and mushrooms. Bring to a boil again. Pour vegetables and sauce over meat and combine.

5. Bake, covered, in preheated 350°F (180°C) toaster oven for 1¾ to 2 hours, or until meat is tender. Stir occasionally during cooking, adding extra water or stock if sauce becomes too dry or thick.

6. Stir in peas. Return to oven and bake, covered, for 10 minutes.

Cabbage and Carrot Slaw

In a large bowl, combine 2 cups (500 mL) shredded cabbage, 2 grated carrots, ½ cup (125 mL) chopped red bell pepper, 2 tbsp (25 mL) olive oil, 2 tbsp (25 mL) lemon juice or rice vinegar, 1 tbsp (15 mL) chopped fresh dillweed and ¼ tsp (1 mL) salt. Makes 3 servings.

Beef Tenderloin with Mustard Horseradish Sauce

As there is little waste and no bone, beef tenderloin is easy to carve. Ask for a section that is about 3 inches (7.5 cm) thick. (If your tenderloin is thicker than this, it may be necessary to lengthen the cooking time by 10 minutes, but use a meat thermometer to be sure.) Serve with sautéed wild mushrooms and mashed potatoes (page 93).

MAKES 4 SERVINGS

Variation

Beef Tenderloin with Wasabi Sauce
Combine ½ cup (125 mL) mayonnaise, 2 tbsp (25 mL) chopped pickled ginger and ½ tsp (2 mL) prepared wasabi (or more to taste). Serve with beef.

2 tbsp	soy sauce	25 mL
1 tbsp	Dijon mustard	15 mL
1 tbsp	olive oil	15 mL
1 tsp	grated lemon zest	5 mL
1	1½-lb (750 g) piece beef tenderloin	1

Mustard Horseradish Sauce

½ cup	mayonnaise	125 mL
3 tbsp	prepared horseradish	45 mL
2 tbsp	Russian-style mustard	25 mL

1. In a small bowl, combine soy sauce, mustard, oil and lemon zest.
2. Place beef in a shallow dish. Rub soy sauce marinade over beef. Let stand at room temperature for 30 minutes.
3. Place beef on broiler rack set over oven pan. Roast in preheated 500°F (260°C) toaster oven for 20 minutes.
4. Reduce heat to 350°F (180°C) and continue to roast for 25 to 30 minutes, or until a meat thermometer registers 140°F (60°C) for medium-rare. Let stand for 10 minutes.
5. Meanwhile, to prepare sauce, in a bowl, stir together mayonnaise, horseradish and mustard. Carve beef and serve with sauce.

Wasabi

Wasabi is a fiery green horseradish root often served with sushi. It comes in tins of powder (to be mixed with water) and tubes of paste. It is available in Asian stores, usually in the Japanese section.

Deli Tuna Melts (page 13)

Fish Tacos (page 14) with
Avocado Corn Salsa (page 65)

Craig's Roast Beef and
Cheese Sliders (page 19)

BBQ Meatballs (page 22)

Vegetable Bean Chili (page 26)
and Cornbread (page 167)

Salmon Satays (page 39)

Salsa, Crab and Cheese Spread (page 48)

Roasted Fish Fillets with
Crumb Topping (page 64)

Homestyle Meatloaf

This old standby is still a big favorite. Instead of ground beef you can use a combination of ground meats such as pork, veal, turkey or chicken. Slice leftovers to serve in sandwiches.

MAKES 6 SERVINGS

1 tbsp	olive oil	15 mL
1	onion, chopped	1
3	cloves garlic, finely chopped	3
1	egg	1
1½ lbs	lean ground beef	750 g
½ cup	fresh breadcrumbs	125 mL
½ cup	ketchup or chili sauce	125 mL
1 tbsp	prepared horseradish	15 mL
1 tbsp	Worcestershire sauce	15 mL
1 tbsp	Dijon mustard	15 mL
½ tsp	dried sage leaves	2 mL
½ tsp	salt	2 mL
¼ tsp	black pepper	1 mL

Topping

¼ cup	ketchup	50 mL
1 tsp	prepared horseradish	5 mL
1 tsp	Dijon mustard	5 mL

1. In a small skillet, heat oil over medium-high heat. Add onion and garlic. Cook, stirring occasionally, for 3 minutes, or until softened.

2. In a large bowl, beat egg. Add ground beef, cooked onion mixture, breadcrumbs, ketchup, horseradish, Worcestershire, mustard, sage, salt and pepper. Mix together thoroughly. Pack into an 8- by 4-inch (1.5 L) loaf pan.

3. For topping, in small bowl, combine ketchup, horseradish and mustard. Spread over top of meatloaf.

4. Bake in preheated 350°F (180°C) toaster oven for 70 to 75 minutes, or until a meat thermometer registers 170°F (75°C). Let stand for 10 to 15 minutes. Pour off any accumulated fat before slicing.

Roast Beef and Potatoes

This will satisfy the meat and potato lovers in your house. For a moist, tender roast, be sure not to overcook it. Starting at a high temperature helps the initial browning and gets the potatoes cooking. Use this combination high-low cooking method for other roasts, checking for doneness with a meat thermometer (see chart, page 10).

Serve this with baby carrots and horseradish.

MAKES 4 SERVINGS

2 tsp	vegetable oil, divided	10 mL
1 tsp	Worcestershire sauce	5 mL
1 tsp	Dijon mustard	5 mL
1	sirloin tip roast (about 2 lbs/1 kg)	1
3	potatoes, peeled and cut in 1½-inch (4 cm) pieces	3
¼ tsp	salt	1 mL
¼ tsp	black pepper	1 mL
Gravy		
1 tbsp	butter	15 mL
1	small onion, chopped	1
1 tbsp	all-purpose flour	15 mL
1 cup	beef stock	250 mL
1 tbsp	tomato paste	15 mL
½ tsp	salt	2 mL
¼ tsp	black pepper	1 mL

1. In a small bowl, combine 1 tsp (5 mL) oil, Worcestershire and mustard. Rub mixture on roast.

2. Place roast in an 8-inch (2 L) square baking dish. Pour in ¾ cup (175 mL) water. Place in preheated 500°F (260°C) toaster oven for 15 minutes.

3. Meanwhile, in a bowl, toss potatoes with remaining 1 tsp (5 mL) oil, salt and pepper.

4. Place potatoes around roast and cook for 15 minutes longer. Reduce heat to 275°F (140°C) and continue to cook for 50 minutes, or until a meat thermometer inserted into roast registers 140°F (60°C) for rare to medium-rare or 160°F (70°C) for medium. Turn potatoes occasionally during cooking.

5. Transfer potatoes and roast to a serving platter, reserving juices, and cover loosely with foil to keep warm while you are making gravy.

6. To make gravy, melt butter in a saucepan over medium heat. Add onion and cook, stirring occasionally, for 4 minutes, or until softened.

7. Stir in flour. Whisk in stock, reserved meat juices and tomato paste. Bring to a boil and cook for 5 minutes, or until slightly thickened (this is not a thick gravy). Add salt and pepper.

8. Slice roast and serve with potatoes and gravy.

A Different Shepherd's Pie

This shepherd's pie contains dried fruit and chutney, reminiscent of bobotie, a traditional dish of South Africa. Don't be put off by the long ingredient list. This goes together easily. You can also add ½ cup (125 mL) corn kernels to the meat mixture or use other ground meats such as lamb, pork, veal, chicken or turkey. Serve it with roasted pears.

MAKES 4 SERVINGS

Make Ahead

Cook potato topping and meat mixture. Cool separately. Once cooled, assemble pie. Cover and refrigerate up to a day before baking.

1½ lbs	potatoes (about 3 medium), peeled and cut in 2-inch (5 cm) pieces	750 g
1	large sweet potato, peeled and cut in 2-inch (5 cm) pieces	1
¼ cup	milk	50 mL
2 tbsp	butter	25 mL
1¼ tsp	salt, divided	6 mL
1 tbsp	vegetable oil	15 mL
1	onion, chopped	1
1 lb	lean ground beef	500 g
½ tsp	curry powder	2 mL
½ tsp	ground ginger	2 mL
2 tbsp	all-purpose flour	25 mL
1 cup	beef stock or chicken stock	250 mL
1	apple, peeled and finely chopped	1
1 cup	grated carrot	250 mL
2 tbsp	chopped dried apricots	25 mL
2 tbsp	mango chutney	25 mL
¼ tsp	black pepper	1 mL

1. In a large saucepan, cook potatoes and sweet potato in plenty of salted boiling water for 20 minutes, or until tender. Drain well. Mash potatoes with milk, butter and ¾ tsp (4 mL) salt.

2. In a large skillet, heat oil over medium-high heat. Add onion and cook, stirring, for 1 minute. Add ground beef and cook, stirring occasionally, for 4 minutes, or until pinkness disappears.

3. Stir in curry powder, ginger and flour and cook, stirring, for 2 minutes.

4. Add stock, apple, carrot, apricots, chutney, remaining $\frac{1}{2}$ tsp (2 mL) salt and pepper. Cook for 4 minutes, stirring, until mixture thickens.

5. Spoon mixture into a lightly greased 8-inch (2 L) square baking dish. Spread mashed potato mixture over meat.

6. Bake in preheated 350°F (180°C) toaster oven for 30 to 35 minutes, or until top is golden and mixture is bubbling at sides.

Roasted Pears

Halve and core 4 ripe Bartlett or Anjou pears. Place pear halves, cut side up, on oven pan (trim a thin slice from rounded sides if necessary to prevent wobbling). Drizzle pears with 1 tbsp (15 mL) olive oil. Sprinkle with 1 tsp (5 mL) chopped fresh marjoram or tarragon (or $\frac{1}{2}$ tsp/2 mL dried), $\frac{1}{4}$ tsp (1 mL) salt and $\frac{1}{4}$ tsp (1 mL) black pepper. Bake in preheated 375°F (190°C) toaster oven for 20 to 25 minutes, or until pears are tender and lightly browned (timing will depend on ripeness of pears). Serve cold or at room temperature. Makes 4 servings.

Meatballs with Teriyaki Sauce

Serve the humble meatball with pasta, mashed potatoes (page 93), stir-fried rice (page 110), in sandwiches or as appetizers. Try one of the other suggested sauces or use your own family recipe.

(page 93), stir-fried rice (page 110)

MAKES 4 TO 5 SERVINGS

Variations

Meatballs with Sweet and Sour Sauce

For sauce, combine ¾ cup (175 mL) ketchup, ½ cup (125 mL) pineapple juice, ¼ cup (50 mL) white vinegar, 2 tbsp (25 mL) packed brown sugar and 1 tbsp (15 mL) soy sauce.

Meatballs with Tomato Sauce

For sauce, combine 1½ cups (375 mL) tomato sauce, 2 minced cloves garlic, 1 chopped small onion and ¼ cup (50 mL) grated Parmesan cheese.

Meatballs with Cranberry Sauce

For sauce, combine 1 cup (250 mL) cranberry sauce, ¼ cup (50 mL) orange juice, ¼ cup (50 mL) red wine vinegar, 2 tbsp (25 mL) packed brown sugar and 2 tsp (10 mL) Dijon mustard.

Meatballs

1 lb	lean ground beef, chicken or turkey	500 g
½ cup	fresh breadcrumbs	125 mL
1	egg, beaten	1
2 tbsp	Worcestershire sauce	25 mL
¼ cup	finely chopped green onion	50 mL
½ tsp	salt	2 mL
½ tsp	black pepper	2 mL

Teriyaki Sauce

½ cup	chicken stock	125 mL
¼ cup	soy sauce	50 mL
¼ cup	rice wine (mirin) or orange juice	50 mL
2 tbsp	granulated sugar	25 mL
1 tbsp	chopped gingerroot	15 mL

1. In a large bowl, combine ground meat, breadcrumbs, egg, Worcestershire, green onion, salt and pepper. Shape mixture into about 25 meatballs (about 1 inch/2.5 cm in diameter). Arrange in a lightly greased 8 inch (2 L) square baking dish.

2. For sauce, in a medium bowl, combine chicken stock, soy sauce, rice wine, sugar and ginger. Pour sauce over meatballs.

3. Bake in preheated 375°F (190°C) toaster oven for 40 minutes, carefully stirring occasionally.

Sausage and Penne Bake

Keep bottled sauces in the cupboard for a last-minute dish like this one. You can also add a 10-oz (300 g) package frozen chopped spinach (defrosted and squeezed dry) with the pasta sauce.

MAKES 4 TO 5 SERVINGS

2 cups	uncooked penne (about 6 oz/175 g)	500 mL
2 tbsp	olive oil	25 mL
1	onion, chopped	1
2	cloves garlic, finely chopped	2
8 oz	sweet Italian sausage, cut in 1-inch (2.5 cm) pieces	250 g
1	24-oz (700 mL) jar tomato pasta sauce	1
1 cup	grated mozzarella cheese	250 mL
2 tbsp	chopped fresh basil or pesto (page 63)	25 mL
2 tbsp	grated Parmesan cheese	25 mL

1. In a large saucepan, cook penne in a large amount of boiling salted water for 8 to 10 minutes, or until just tender. Drain, reserving $3/4$ cup (175 mL) pasta water. (You should have about 3 cups/750 mL cooked penne.)

2. Meanwhile, in a large skillet, heat oil over medium-high heat. Add onion, garlic and sausage. Cook, stirring occasionally, for 8 minutes, or until sausage is no longer pink. Remove from heat.

3. Stir in pasta sauce, mozzarella, basil, cooked pasta and reserved pasta water. Transfer to a lightly greased 8-cup (2 L) baking dish. Sprinkle with Parmesan cheese.

4. Bake in preheated 375°F (190°C) toaster oven for 25 to 30 minutes, or until hot and bubbling.

Chili Cheese Dog Bake

A friend of a friend kept asking me for a recipe for chili cheese dogs. He used to love them when he worked at a restaurant as a teenager. Keep the ingredients on hand for this convenient one-dish version that can be rounded out with a green salad. Good-quality canned chili is available in most supermarkets.

MAKES 3 SERVINGS

1½ cups	homemade (page 26 or 105) or storebought chili	375 mL
½ cup	chili sauce or tomato salsa	125 mL
3	wieners, cut in 1½-inch (4 cm) pieces	3
1 cup	grated Cheddar cheese	250 mL
3	hot dog rolls or crusty rolls	3

1. In a 6-cup (1.5 L) casserole (with lid), combine chili, chili sauce and wieners.
2. Bake, covered, in preheated 400°F (200°C) toaster oven for 20 minutes.
3. Sprinkle with cheese and return to oven. Bake, uncovered, for 10 minutes, or until cheese melts and mixture is bubbling at edges.
4. Place rolls on rack and bake for 5 minutes or until heated through. Spoon chili cheese bake over buns or serve in bowls with buns alongside.

Bill's Oven Chili

My friend Bill makes big batches of chili either for catering or to freeze in family-sized portions. This is a scaled-down version of his recipe.

MAKES 6 SERVINGS

2 tbsp	olive oil	25 mL
1	onion, chopped	1
8 oz	lean ground beef	250 g
1	14-oz (398 mL) can baked beans	1
1	19-oz (540 mL) can red kidney beans, rinsed and drained	1
1	14-oz (398 mL) can diced tomatoes, with juices (about 1¾ cups/425 mL)	1
1½ tsp	chili powder	7 mL
½ tsp	salt	2 mL
½ tsp	garlic salt or garlic powder	2 mL
½ tsp	black pepper	2 mL
¼ tsp	hot red pepper flakes	1 mL

1. In a large skillet, heat oil over medium-high heat. Add onion and cook, stirring, for 2 minutes, or until softened.

2. Add beef. Cook, breaking up meat, for 6 minutes, or until no longer pink.

3. Add baked beans, kidney beans, tomatoes and juices, chili powder, salt, garlic salt, pepper and hot pepper flakes. Bring to a boil. Transfer to a shallow 8-cup (2 L) casserole (with lid).

4. Bake, covered, in preheated 325°F (160°F) toaster oven for 1 to 1¼ hours, or until thickened yet still juicy. Stir occasionally during baking.

Stuffed Peppers

Shop for peppers that do not have too many ridges, so they will not topple over during cooking. Serve these as a starter or as a main course.

MAKES 2 TO 4 SERVINGS

Make Ahead

Cool filling before stuffing peppers. Assembled dish can be prepared, covered and refrigerated up to 8 hours before baking.

2	red, yellow or green bell peppers, seeded and halved lengthwise	2
1 tbsp	olive oil	15 mL
1	onion, chopped	1
2	cloves garlic, finely chopped	2
8 oz	Italian sausage meat (removed from casings)	250 g
1 cup	cooked macaroni	250 mL
¾ cup	tomato sauce	175 mL
½ tsp	dried oregano leaves	2 mL
½ tsp	salt	2 mL
¼ tsp	black pepper	1 mL
1 cup	grated mozzarella or Asiago cheese	250 mL

1. Arrange peppers cut side up in an 8-inch (2 L) square baking dish.
2. In a large skillet, heat olive oil over medium-high heat. Add onion and garlic. Cook, stirring occasionally, for 3 minutes.
3. Add sausage meat to skillet and cook, breaking up chunks, for 6 minutes, or until pinkness disappears. Transfer to a large bowl.
4. Add macaroni, tomato sauce, oregano, salt and pepper to sausage mixture and stir together.
5. Spoon mixture into pepper halves. Pour ¼ cup (50 mL) water into bottom of pan.
6. Cover baking dish tightly with foil. Bake in preheated 400°F (200°C) toaster oven for 30 minutes.
7. Sprinkle peppers with cheese. Bake, uncovered, for 8 to 10 minutes longer, or until cheese melts and peppers are soft yet still hold their shape.

Stuffed Pork Loin Roast with Cranapple Sauce

The beauty of this roast is that it is tender and oven-ready. Many butcher shops have their own house stuffing, and they will cut a roast that is the size you need.

The cranapple sauce goes well with chicken, turkey and ham dishes, or use it in sandwiches. The raspberry juice concentrate gives the sauce a bright red color. Freeze leftover concentrate to use in salad dressings (add 1 tbsp/15 mL to a vinaigrette), desserts or in a punch.

MAKES 5 TO 6 SERVINGS

Make Ahead

Sauce can be cooked, covered and refrigerated for up to a week.

Variation

Pork Loin Roast with Chipotle Rub
Add 2 tsp (10 mL) chipotle puree (see box, page 90) to rub for roast.

Pork

2 tbsp	orange juice concentrate	25 mL
1 tbsp	Dijon mustard	15 mL
1	clove garlic, minced	1
½ tsp	dried sage leaves	2 mL
1	oven-ready stuffed pork loin roast (about 3 lbs/1.5 kg)	1

Cranapple Sauce

1 lb	fresh or frozen cranberries	500 g
2	apples, peeled and chopped	2
½ cup	granulated sugar	125 mL
½ cup	raspberry juice concentrate, or orange juice	125 mL

1. In a small bowl, combine orange juice concentrate, mustard, garlic and sage. Rub over roast.
2. Place roast in an 8-inch (2 L) square baking pan, fat side up. Add ¼ cup (50 mL) water to pan.
3. Bake in preheated 350°F (180°C) toaster oven for 1¾ hours, or until a meat thermometer inserted in meat (not in stuffing) registers 160°F (70°C). Add extra water if pan becomes dry.
4. Meanwhile, to prepare sauce, combine cranberries, apples, sugar and raspberry juice concentrate in a saucepan. Bring to a boil, reduce heat and simmer, uncovered, for 12 to 15 minutes, or until apples are cooked and mixture is saucelike. Stir frequently during cooking. Cool.
5. Remove roast from oven, cover loosely with foil and let stand for 10 minutes before carving. Serve roast with sauce.

Sweet and Sour Pork

This is a version of a dish that my mother always made for birthday parties and company, only she used spareribs. Although she prepared it in large quantities, the recipe has been adjusted for easy baking in the toaster oven. I was usually assigned the task of making fried rice (page 110) to accompany it. Serve with a green salad or a fresh vegetable tray.

MAKES 3 TO 4 SERVINGS

1	14-oz (398 mL) can pineapple chunks, with juices	1
½ cup	tomato sauce	125 mL
¼ cup	diced sweet pickle	50 mL
¼ cup	cider vinegar	50 mL
2 tbsp	packed brown sugar	25 mL
1 tbsp	cornstarch	15 mL
1 tbsp	soy sauce	15 mL
1 tbsp	Dijon mustard	15 mL
1 tbsp	vegetable oil	15 mL
1 lb	boneless pork loin or pork leg roast, cut in ½-inch (1 cm) pieces	500 g
1	onion, thinly sliced	1
1	red bell pepper, seeded and cut in ½-inch (1 cm) pieces	1
2 tsp	finely chopped gingerroot	10 mL

1. In a bowl, combine pineapple chunks and juices with tomato sauce, pickle, vinegar, brown sugar, cornstarch, soy sauce and mustard.

2. In a large skillet, heat oil over medium-high heat. Add pork and cook, stirring occasionally, until brown, about 6 minutes. Transfer to an 8-cup (2 L) casserole (with lid). Add pineapple mixture, onion, red pepper and ginger. Stir to combine.

3. Bake, covered, in preheated 350°F (180°C) toaster oven for 1 to 1¼ hours, or until pork is very tender. Stir occasionally during cooking.

Southwestern Spareribs

The smoky chipotle peppers and sweet chili sauce combine for a full-flavored dish. Serve with cornbread (page 167).

If sweet-and-sour-cut spareribs (also called button ribs or center cut pork ribs) are not available at the meat counter, ask the butcher to cut longer ribs into narrow strips.

MAKES 3 SERVINGS

1½ lbs	sweet-and-sour-cut pork spareribs	750 g
1½ cups	storebought or homemade chili sauce	375 mL
2 tbsp	honey	25 mL
2 tbsp	lime juice	25 mL
1 tbsp	coarse-grain mustard	15 mL
1 tbsp	chipotle puree (see box, page 90)	15 mL
1 tbsp	Worcestershire sauce	15 mL
1 tsp	ground cumin	5 mL
½ tsp	salt	2 mL
½ tsp	black pepper	2 mL
2 tbsp	chopped fresh cilantro	25 mL

1. Cut ribs into serving portions. Place in an 8-cup (2 L) casserole (with lid).

2. In a bowl, combine chili sauce, honey, lime juice, mustard, chipotles, Worcestershire, cumin, salt and pepper. Pour sauce over ribs.

3. Bake, covered, in preheated 350°F (180°C) toaster oven for 1 hour, basting occasionally with sauce. Remove cover and bake for 30 minutes longer, or until pork is very tender. Sprinkle with cilantro before serving.

Thai Pork Tenderloin

An easy preparation for a tender, slightly exotic, full-flavored pork tenderloin. Serve hot with steamed broccoli and stir-fried rice or chill and slice thinly for sandwiches, salads or meat trays. For a less spicy version, reduce the sweet Asian chili sauce to 1 tbsp (15 mL).

MAKES 5 TO 6 SERVINGS

2	cloves garlic, minced	2
1 tbsp	finely chopped gingerroot	15 mL
2 tbsp	finely chopped fresh cilantro	25 mL
3 tbsp	hoisin sauce	45 mL
2 tbsp	lime juice or lemon juice	25 mL
1 tbsp	fish sauce or soy sauce	15 mL
1 tbsp	roasted sesame oil	15 mL
2 tbsp	sweet Asian chili sauce (page 51)	25 mL
2	pork tenderloins (about 12 oz/ 375 g each)	2

1. In a small bowl, combine garlic, ginger, cilantro, hoisin, lime juice, fish sauce, sesame oil and sweet Asian chili sauce.

2. Arrange tenderloins in a single layer in a dish just large enough to hold pork. Pour sauce over meat, turning tenderloins to coat. Cover and refrigerate for 1 to 24 hours.

3. Arrange tenderloins with sauce on parchment paper cut to fit oven pan. Discard any extra marinade. Bake in preheated 350°F (180°C) toaster oven for 30 to 35 minutes, or until just a hint of pink remains in pork. Let stand for 5 minutes, then slice on the diagonal.

Stir-fried Rice

Heat 2 tbsp (25 mL) vegetable oil in a wok or large saucepan over medium-high heat. Add 1 thinly sliced onion, 2 thinly sliced stalks celery and 1 cup (250 mL) sliced mushrooms. Stir-fry for 4 minutes.

Add 3 cups (750 mL) cold cooked rice and ½ cup (125 mL) fresh or frozen green peas. Stir-fry for 6 to 8 minutes, or until rice is heated through.

Add 2 beaten eggs and continue to stir-fry for 4 minutes, or until eggs are cooked. Stir in 2 tbsp (25 mL) soy sauce and 2 chopped green onions. Makes 5 to 6 servings.

Crusted Pork Chops
with Tomato Salsa

When cooking pork chops without a sauce, it is important not to overcook them, as they can easily become dry. Cook just until a hint of pink remains in pork.

These chops are an easy answer when you are looking for a quick supper. Watch for weekly specials on pork chops at supermarkets and stock your freezer. Serve with the tomato salsa or try other salsas (page 65) or cranapple sauce (page 107).

MAKES 4 SERVINGS

2 tbsp	cornmeal	25 mL
2 tbsp	grated Parmesan cheese	25 mL
2 tbsp	all-purpose flour	25 mL
1 tsp	paprika (preferably smoked)	5 mL
½ tsp	salt	2 mL
½ cup	buttermilk or unflavored yogurt	125 mL
4	boneless pork loin chops (about 6 oz/175 g each)	4

Tomato Salsa

2	tomatoes, seeded and chopped (about 1¾ cups/425 mL)	2
2	green onions, chopped	2
2 tbsp	chopped fresh basil	25 mL
2 tbsp	lime juice or lemon juice	25 mL
1 tbsp	balsamic vinegar	15 mL
1 tbsp	olive oil	15 mL
¼ tsp	salt	1 mL
¼ tsp	black pepper	1 mL

1. Combine cornmeal, cheese, flour, paprika and salt in a shallow dish. Pour buttermilk into a separate shallow dish.

2. Dip chops in buttermilk, then in cornmeal mixture, turning to coat both sides. (Discard any excess buttermilk and cornmeal mixture.) Place chops on lightly greased broiler rack placed over oven pan.

3. Bake in preheated 375°F (190°C) toaster oven for 10 minutes. Turn chops and continue to bake for 10 to 15 minutes, or until just a hint of pink remains in pork.

4. Meanwhile, to prepare salsa, in a bowl, combine tomatoes, green onions, basil, lime juice, vinegar, oil, salt and pepper. Serve with pork chops.

Braised Veal
with Sweet Potatoes

This aromatic sauce contains orange and cumin, which go well with the delicate veal. Serve with couscous (page 59) and garnish with orange sections.

MAKES 4 SERVINGS

2 tbsp	vegetable oil, divided	25 mL
1	onion, chopped	1
2	carrots, chopped	2
1	stalk celery, chopped	1
4 tbsp	all-purpose flour, divided	60 mL
¼ tsp	salt	1 mL
¼ tsp	black pepper	1 mL
1 lb	stewing veal, cut in 1½-inch (4 cm) cubes	500 g
2 cups	chicken stock	500 mL
¼ cup	orange juice concentrate	50 mL
2 tbsp	tomato paste	25 mL
½ tsp	ground cumin	2 mL
2	sweet potatoes, peeled and cut in 1-inch (2.5 cm) pieces	2

1. In a large skillet, heat 1 tbsp (15 mL) vegetable oil over medium-high heat. Add onion, carrots and celery. Cook, stirring occasionally, until lightly colored, about 4 minutes. Transfer to an 8-cup (2 L) casserole (with lid).

2. Meanwhile, in a shallow dish, combine 3 tbsp (45 mL) flour with salt and pepper. Dust veal with seasoned flour.

3. Add remaining 1 tbsp (15 mL) oil to skillet. Add veal and cook for 6 to 8 minutes, or until browned on all sides. Add veal to vegetables in casserole.

4. Add stock, remaining 1 tbsp (15 mL) flour, orange juice concentrate, tomato paste and cumin to skillet. Stir, scraping caramelized bits from bottom of pan, and bring to a boil. Pour over veal and vegetables.

5. Bake, covered, in preheated 350°F (180°C) toaster oven for 1 hour, stirring twice during cooking time.

6. Add sweet potatoes to casserole and stir in. Cover and cook for 35 to 40 minutes longer, or until veal and potatoes are tender.

Herbed Butterflied Leg of Lamb

This is a terrific dish, especially in early summer, when fresh herbs first appear in the markets. Serve it with steamed asparagus or fiddleheads followed by fresh strawberries or a lemon dessert.

Look for small butterflied legs of lamb in the fresh or frozen meat department. Some supermarkets now sell lamb boned and encased in a netting. To butterfly, simply remove the netting and cut partway through the roast to open it up, or ask the butcher to do this for you.

Use any leftover lamb in pita sandwiches.

MAKES 4 TO 5 SERVINGS

½ cup	packed basil leaves	125 mL
½ cup	packed parsley leaves	125 mL
3	green onions, coarsely chopped	3
2	cloves garlic, chopped	2
2 tbsp	Russian-style mustard	25 mL
2 tbsp	balsamic vinegar	25 mL
2 tbsp	olive oil	25 mL
1	3-lb (1.5 kg) butterflied leg of lamb, trimmed	1

1. In a food processor, combine basil, parsley, green onions and garlic. Process until finely chopped.
2. Add mustard, vinegar and oil to food processor and blend in.
3. Place lamb in a shallow dish. Spoon marinade over lamb and turn to coat all sides. Cover and marinate, refrigerated, for 3 hours or overnight.
4. Arrange lamb fat side up on lightly greased broiler rack set over oven pan.
5. Roast in preheated 375°F (190°C) toaster oven for 25 to 30 minutes, or until meat thermometer registers 140°F (60°C) for medium-rare. Cover loosely with foil and let stand for 5 to 10 minutes before carving across the grain.

Honey Mustard Lamb Chops

For a special dinner for two, lamb chops are easy to broil in the toaster oven. Serve with a tomato salsa (page 111), and add 1 tbsp (15 mL) chopped fresh mint. For a vegetable accompaniment, make a colorful pepper salad (page 137) ahead and serve with baked potatoes (page 130). Bake the potatoes just before broiling the chops (cover the potatoes with foil to keep them hot).

MAKES 2 SERVINGS

1 tbsp	coarse-grain mustard	15 mL
1 tbsp	honey	15 mL
1 tbsp	olive oil	15 mL
1 tsp	chopped fresh rosemary, or ½ tsp (2 mL) dried	5 mL
4 to 6	lean lamb chops, trimmed, 1 inch (2.5 cm) thick (about 1 lb/500 g total)	4 to 6
¼ tsp	salt	1 mL
¼ tsp	black pepper	1 mL

1. In a small bowl, combine mustard, honey, oil and rosemary.
2. Arrange lamb chops on lightly greased broiler rack set over oven pan. Spoon half of glaze over chops.
3. Place lamb under preheated toaster oven broiler (check your manufacturer's manual to see whether the oven door should be left ajar during broiling). Broil for 6 to 7 minutes. Turn and spoon remaining glaze over chops. Broil for 6 to 7 minutes longer for rare. Sprinkle with salt and pepper.

Meatless Main Courses

Old-fashioned
Macaroni and Cheese

This old-time favorite has a golden, crispy crust. Don't save it just for family meals. Your guests will love something this homey and delicious.

MAKES 4 TO 6 SERVINGS

1½ cups	uncooked macaroni (about 6 oz/175 g)	375 mL
2 tbsp	butter	25 mL
1	onion, chopped	1
2 tbsp	all-purpose flour	25 mL
2 cups	milk	500 mL
¾ tsp	salt	4 mL
½ tsp	dry mustard	2 mL
¼ tsp	paprika	1 mL
¼ tsp	black pepper	1 mL
1½ cups	grated Cheddar cheese	375 mL
1 cup	fresh breadcrumbs	250 mL
2 tbsp	butter, melted	25 mL

1. In a large saucepan, cook macaroni in a large amount of boiling salted water for 8 to 10 minutes, or until just tender. Drain well. (You should have about 3 cups/750 mL cooked macaroni.)

2. Meanwhile, melt butter in a large saucepan over medium heat. Add onion and cook, stirring occasionally, for 3 minutes, or until softened. Add flour and cook, stirring, for 3 minutes.

3. Whisk in milk. Bring sauce to a boil, reduce heat and simmer, stirring occasionally, for 6 minutes. Remove from heat.

4. Season sauce with salt, mustard, paprika and pepper.

5. Stir in drained macaroni and cheese. Spoon macaroni into a lightly greased 6-cup (1.5 L) shallow baking dish.

6. In a small bowl, stir together breadcrumbs and melted butter. Sprinkle breadcrumbs over macaroni.

7. Bake in preheated 350°F (180°C) toaster oven for 30 to 35 minutes, or until golden and bubbling.

Rotini with Cheese and Corn

Use rotini (spiral-shaped pasta), penne or rotelle (wagon-wheels) in this popular pasta dish. Serve with steamed broccoli or sautéed green beans (page 75).

MAKES 4 SERVINGS

2 cups	uncooked rotini (about 6 oz/175 g)	500 mL
2 tbsp	butter	25 mL
1	onion, chopped	1
1	stalk celery, chopped	1
1 tsp	curry powder	5 mL
2 tbsp	all-purpose flour	25 mL
2 cups	milk	500 mL
1 cup	fresh or frozen and defrosted corn kernels	250 mL
1 cup	grated Swiss cheese	250 mL
1/2 cup	grated Cheddar cheese	125 mL
3/4 tsp	salt	4 mL
1/2 tsp	black pepper	2 mL
1/2 cup	fresh breadcrumbs	125 mL
2 tbsp	grated Parmesan cheese	25 mL

1. Cook rotini in a large amount of boiling salted water for 8 to 10 minutes, or until just tender. Drain well. (You should have about 3 cups/750 mL cooked rotini.)

2. Meanwhile, melt butter in a large saucepan over medium heat. Add onion and celery and cook, stirring occasionally, for 4 minutes, or until softened.

3. Stir in curry powder and cook for 30 seconds. Add flour and cook, stirring, for 3 minutes.

4. Whisk in milk. Bring sauce to a boil, reduce heat and simmer, stirring occasionally, for 6 minutes. Remove from heat and stir in drained rotini, corn, Swiss and Cheddar cheese, salt and pepper.

5. Spoon into a lightly greased 6-cup (1.5 L) shallow baking dish. Sprinkle with breadcrumbs and Parmesan.

6. Bake in preheated 350°F (180°C) toaster oven for 35 minutes, or until golden and bubbling.

Spaghetti Pie

This recipe evolved when I had leftover cooked spaghetti and cottage cheese in the fridge. Now it is one of my favorite one-dish meals. Serve it with a green salad. Leftovers are good, slightly warmed, the next day.

For a non-vegetarian version, add ½ cup (125 mL) diced ham or prosciutto.

MAKES 4 TO 6 SERVINGS

6 oz	uncooked spaghetti	175 g
1 cup	small-curd cottage cheese	250 mL
1 cup	tomato sauce or pasta sauce	250 mL
2	eggs, beaten	2
½ cup	grated Fontina cheese	125 mL
½ cup	grated Swiss cheese	125 mL
¾ tsp	salt	4 mL
¾ tsp	chili powder	4 mL
¼ tsp	dried oregano leaves	1 mL
¼ tsp	black pepper	1 mL
2 tbsp	grated Parmesan cheese	25 mL

1. In a large saucepan, cook spaghetti in a large amount of boiling salted water for 8 minutes, or until just tender. Drain well and return to saucepan. (You should have about 2½ cups/625 mL cooked spaghetti.)

2. Add cottage cheese, tomato sauce, eggs, Fontina and Swiss cheese, salt, chili powder, oregano and pepper. Combine thoroughly.

3. Turn into a well-greased 9-inch (23 cm) pie plate. Sprinkle with Parmesan.

4. Bake in preheated 350°F (180°C) toaster oven for 35 minutes. Let stand for 10 minutes before cutting into wedges.

Pasta with Cherry Tomatoes and Feta

There are so many different varieties of cherry tomatoes now, from tiny red, yellow or orange tomatoes to the teardrop or grape varieties. Some of them are so sweet that they almost seem like a vegetable candy. Roasting them in the toaster oven highlights the natural sweetness even more.

The tomatoes and cheese could also be served separately as an appetizer.

MAKES 3 TO 4 SERVINGS

1½ cups	small cherry tomatoes	375 mL
3 tbsp	olive oil, divided	45 mL
¼ tsp	salt	1 mL
¼ tsp	black pepper	1 mL
8 oz	uncooked penne	250 g
8 oz	feta cheese, broken in small pieces (about 1¼ cups/300 mL)	250 g
2 tbsp	chopped fresh basil	25 mL
2 tbsp	chopped fresh chives	25 mL
1 tsp	chopped fresh oregano or rosemary	5 mL

1. In a bowl, toss tomatoes with 2 tbsp (25 mL) olive oil, salt and pepper. Place in an 8-inch (2 L) square baking dish.

2. Bake in preheated 400°F (200°C) toaster oven for 20 to 25 minutes, or until softened and lightly browned. (Timing will depend on size of tomatoes.) Tomatoes will collapse slightly and skins may pop.

3. Meanwhile, cook penne in a large saucepan of boiling salted water for 8 to 10 minutes, or until just tender. Drain well. (You should have about 3 cups/750 mL cooked penne.)

4. Toss pasta with tomatoes, feta and remaining 1 tbsp (15 mL) oil. Sprinkle with basil, chives and oregano.

Mexican Tortilla Pie

Mexican flavors are festive, vibrant and exciting, and this is a quick dish to assemble if you have a few key ingredients already on the shelf. Serve with dishes of sour cream, shredded lettuce, diced tomatoes and guacamole alongside.

MAKES 6 SERVINGS

Make Ahead

Pie can be assembled up to 2 hours before baking.

1	19-oz (540 mL) can kidney beans or black beans, rinsed and drained	1
1	12-oz (341 mL) can corn kernels, drained, or 1½ cups (375 mL) frozen and defrosted	1
2 cups	tomato salsa, divided	500 mL
¼ cup	chopped fresh cilantro	50 mL
1	jalapeño pepper, seeded and chopped	1
1 tsp	chili powder	5 mL
½ tsp	ground cumin	2 mL
2 cups	grated Monterey Jack or Cheddar cheese, divided	500 mL
4	9-inch (23 cm) flour tortillas	4

1. In a large bowl, combine beans, corn, 1½ cups (375 mL) salsa, cilantro, jalapeño, chili powder, cumin and 1½ cups (375 mL) cheese.

2. Place 1 tortilla on bottom of a lightly greased 9-inch (23 cm) pie plate. Top with one-third of bean mixture. Repeat layers two more times. Top with remaining tortilla.

3. Spread remaining ½ cup (125 mL) salsa over top and sprinkle with remaining ½ cup (125 mL) cheese.

4. Bake in preheated 350°F (180°C) toaster oven for 30 to 35 minutes, or until heated through and cheese has melted. Let stand for 10 minutes before cutting into wedges.

Lentil and Chèvre Casserole

Another great vegetarian dish. Serve hot or at room temperature. It also works well as a side dish with roast lamb leg and cold sliced ham.

You could use chickpeas, black beans or Romano beans instead of the lentils.

MAKES 2 TO 3 SERVINGS

Make Ahead

Cool onions, then assemble casserole. Cover and refrigerate up to a day before baking.

2 tbsp	olive oil, divided	25 mL
1	onion, chopped	1
2	cloves garlic, finely chopped	2
1	19-oz (540 mL) can green lentils, rinsed and drained, or 2 cups (500 mL) cooked lentils	1
½ cup	tomato sauce	125 mL
¾ cup	crumbled chèvre (goat cheese)	175 mL
2 tbsp	chopped fresh parsley	25 mL
1 tbsp	chopped fresh rosemary, or ½ tsp (2 mL) dried	15 mL
½ tsp	salt	2 mL
½ cup	fresh breadcrumbs	125 mL

1. In a small skillet, heat 1 tbsp (15 mL) oil over medium-high heat. Add onion and garlic. Cook, stirring, for about 3 minutes, or until softened.
2. In a large bowl, combine cooked onion mixture, lentils, tomato sauce, chèvre, parsley, rosemary and salt. Turn into a lightly greased 6-cup (1.5 L) baking dish.
3. In a small bowl, combine breadcrumbs and remaining 1 tbsp (15 mL) oil. Sprinkle over lentils.
4. Bake in preheated 350°F (180°C) toaster oven for 25 minutes, or until cheese melts and lentils are hot.

Brown Rice and Lentil Bake

This dish can be baked, refrigerated and reheated. To reheat, let stand at room temperature for 30 minutes. Stir in ¼ cup (50 mL) water, cover and reheat in preheated 300°F (150°C) toaster oven for 25 minutes, or until heated through.

MAKES 4 SERVINGS

2 tbsp	olive oil	25 mL
1	onion, chopped	1
½ cup	chopped carrot	125 mL
2	cloves garlic, finely chopped	2
¾ cup	uncooked brown rice, rinsed and drained	175 mL
½ cup	uncooked green lentils, rinsed and drained	125 mL
2 cups	vegetable stock or water	500 mL
½ cup	tomato juice	125 mL
¾ tsp	salt	4 mL
½ tsp	black pepper	2 mL
¼ tsp	ground cumin	1 mL
½ cup	sunflower seeds	125 mL
¼ cup	chopped green onion	50 mL

1. In a large saucepan, heat oil over medium-high heat. Add onion, carrot and garlic. Cook for 4 minutes, stirring occasionally, until softened.

2. Add rice, lentils, stock, tomato juice, salt, pepper and cumin to saucepan and bring to a boil. Transfer to a 6-cup (1.5 L) casserole (with lid).

3. Bake, covered, in preheated 350°F (180°C) toaster oven for 45 to 50 minutes, or until rice is tender and liquid is absorbed. Stir in sunflower seeds and green onion before serving.

Chickpeas in Tomato Sauce

Used in spreads, salads, soups and stews, chickpeas are a rich source of fiber. Serve this with flatbread or rice.

MAKES 4 TO 5 SERVINGS

Make Ahead

Dish can be assembled, covered and refrigerated up to a day before baking.

2 tbsp	olive oil	25 mL
1	onion, chopped	1
1	stalk celery, chopped	1
½ cup	chopped carrot	125 mL
2 cups	tomato sauce	500 mL
½ tsp	salt	2 mL
½ tsp	black pepper	2 mL
½ tsp	dried thyme leaves	2 mL
¼ tsp	hot red pepper flakes	1 mL
1	19-oz (398 mL) can chickpeas, rinsed and drained	1
½ cup	fresh breadcrumbs	125 mL
½ cup	crumbled feta or chèvre (goat cheese)	125 mL

1. In a large skillet, heat oil over medium-high heat. Add onion, celery and carrot. Cook for 4 minutes, or until softened, stirring occasionally.
2. Add tomato sauce, salt, pepper, thyme and hot pepper flakes. Bring to a boil and remove from heat.
3. Stir in chickpeas. Spoon into a lightly greased 6-cup (1.5 L) baking dish.
4. Sprinkle breadcrumbs and cheese over top.
5. Bake in preheated 375°F (190°C) toaster oven for 30 minutes, or until bubbling and golden. Serve hot or at room temperature.

Sweet and Sour Tofu

Tofu on its own has little taste, but it will absorb a sauce with lots of flavor. This one will give it some pizzazz. Serve it with rice and a cucumber salad.

MAKES 3 TO 4 SERVINGS

Make Ahead

Dish can be assembled, covered and refrigerated up to a day ahead.

1	12-oz (350 g) package extra-firm tofu, rinsed, patted dry and cut in ½-inch (1 cm) slices	1
½ cup	ketchup or tomato sauce	125 mL
¼ cup	orange juice or pineapple juice	50 mL
2 tbsp	soy sauce	25 mL
2 tbsp	rice vinegar or lemon juice	25 mL
2 tbsp	packed brown sugar or maple syrup	25 mL
1 tsp	Dijon mustard	5 mL
½ tsp	roasted sesame oil	2 mL
¼ tsp	hot red pepper sauce	1 mL
2 tbsp	finely chopped fresh cilantro	25 mL
1	green onion, finely chopped	1

1. Arrange tofu in a single layer in a lightly greased 8-inch (2 L) square baking dish.
2. In a small bowl, combine ketchup, orange juice, soy sauce, vinegar, sugar, mustard, sesame oil and hot pepper sauce. Pour over tofu, lifting slices so sauce runs underneath.
3. Bake in preheated 350°F (180°C) toaster oven for 25 minutes, or until juices are bubbling at edges.
4. Sprinkle with cilantro and green onion. Let stand for 5 minutes before serving.

Cucumber Salad

In a large bowl, combine 1 thinly sliced small English cucumber, 2 chopped green onions, 3 tbsp (45 mL) rice vinegar, 1 tsp (5 mL) granulated sugar and a pinch of salt. Let stand at room temperature for 20 minutes, tossing occasionally. Makes about 2 cups (500 mL).

Corn and Salsa Quesadilla

Quesadillas are a versatile replacement for the traditional sandwich. For a variation, omit the corn and add 2 tbsp (25 mL) diced roasted red pepper (page 40). You could also add 2 tbsp (25 mL) slightly mashed black beans, or use chèvre (goat cheese) or sliced Brie instead of Monterey Jack. For a non-vegetarian version, add ¼ cup (50 mL) diced cooked chicken. Double or triple the recipe and cook the quesadillas one at a time, sharing the first while the next one is cooking.

MAKES 1 SERVING

2	6-inch (15 cm) flour tortillas	2
2 tbsp	tomato salsa or pasta sauce	25 mL
2 tbsp	fresh or frozen and defrosted corn kernels	25 mL
1	green onion, chopped	1
1 tbsp	chopped fresh cilantro or parsley	15 mL
¼ cup	grated Monterey Jack or mozzarella cheese	50 mL

1. Spread one tortilla with salsa, corn, green onion, cilantro and cheese. Top with remaining tortilla, pressing together lightly.

2. Place quesadilla on oven pan. Bake in preheated 400°F (200°C) toaster oven for 8 minutes, or until hot. Remove to cutting board and let stand for 3 minutes before cutting into wedges.

Portobello Mushroom Burgers

Although not a complete protein, portobello mushrooms are a popular item on vegetarian menus, perhaps because of their meaty texture and full flavor. Because of their size, they are impressive served on their own with various seasonings, and restaurants sometimes include them as a main course, with the mushroom "pretending" to be a filet mignon. However they are served, they are a great addition to any menu. Dress your burger with your favorite condiments.

You can use other cheeses, such as crumbled blue or Gorgonzola (use about ½ cup/125 mL). The mushrooms can also be served as a side dish with meat, poultry or fish.

MAKES 4 BURGERS

4	large portobello mushrooms, (about 4 inches/10 cm in diameter), stemmed	4
⅓ cup	basil pesto (page 63) or Italian vinaigrette	75 mL
4	slices Asiago or Fontina cheese	4
4	Kaiser, onion or hamburger rolls	4
4	thin slices sweet onion	4
4	slices tomato	4
8	arugula leaves	8

1. Place mushrooms round side up on broiler rack set over oven pan. Spoon half of pesto over mushrooms. Broil mushrooms under preheated toaster oven broiler for 6 minutes. (Check your manufacturer's manual to see whether oven door should be left open during broiling.)
2. Turn mushrooms and spoon remaining pesto over top. Broil for 4 minutes. Top with cheese slices and broil for 2 minutes longer.
3. Remove mushrooms from oven. Place buns on rack and bake at 350°F (180°C) for 3 to 4 minutes, or until heated through.
4. Assemble burgers with onion slices, tomato slices and arugula.

Open-face Med Sandwich

When you eat this sandwich you can practically imagine yourself in a café in Italy or the south of France. Try to find baguettes or rolls that have some texture.

MAKES 2 SANDWICHES

1	6-inch (15 cm) baguette or roll, sliced lengthwise	1
1 tbsp	olive oil	15 mL
1	6-oz (170 mL) jar marinated artichoke hearts, drained and chopped	1
2	anchovy fillets, finely chopped	2
1	plum tomato, chopped	1
1/4 cup	crumbled chèvre (goat cheese) or feta	50 mL
2 tbsp	chopped black or green olives	25 mL
2 tsp	drained capers	10 mL
1 tsp	chopped fresh thyme, or 1/2 tsp (2 mL) dried	5 mL
1/2 tsp	black pepper	2 mL

1. Place bread cut side up on oven pan. Remove some of bread to form cavities for filling. Brush bread with olive oil.

2. In a bowl, combine artichokes, anchovies, tomato, cheese, olives, capers, thyme and pepper. Spoon filling into cavities.

3. Bake in preheated 400°F (200°C) toaster oven for 6 to 8 minutes, or until mixture is hot and cheese is soft.

Zucchini and Feta Flan

Similar to a frittata, this flan has a mild flavor enhanced by dill and feta. Serve it with tomatoes and black olives. Serve any leftovers on a salad plate or in a sandwich.

You can use 2 cups (500 mL) diced asparagus instead of the zucchini, replace the feta with grated Cheddar or Swiss cheese, or add $\frac{1}{2}$ cup (125 mL) chopped smoked salmon or ham to this recipe.

MAKES 4 TO 6 SERVINGS

2 tbsp	butter	25 mL
1	onion, chopped	1
2	small zucchini (about 4 oz/125 g each), diced	2
3	eggs	3
1¼ cups	milk	300 mL
½ cup	fresh breadcrumbs	125 mL
2	green onions, chopped	2
1 tbsp	chopped fresh dillweed	15 mL
½ tsp	salt	2 mL
¼ tsp	black pepper	1 mL
1 cup	crumbled feta cheese	250 mL

1. In a medium skillet, melt butter over medium heat. Add onion and zucchini. Cook, stirring often, for 8 minutes, or until zucchini and onion are tender and slightly golden and moisture has evaporated.

2. In a large bowl, beat eggs. Add milk, breadcrumbs, green onions, dill, salt, pepper, feta and zucchini mixture. Pour into a lightly greased 8-inch (2 L) square baking dish.

3. Bake in preheated 350°F (180°C) toaster oven for 35 to 40 minutes, or until eggs are set in center. Let stand for 5 minutes before serving.

Vegetables and Side Dishes

Stuffed Baked Potatoes

Potatoes bake beautifully in the toaster oven. Serve these cheesy herb-stuffed potatoes with cold meats, poultry or fish, or just with a salad for a light meal.

MAKES 4 TO 6 SERVINGS

Variations

Baked Potatoes with Mexican Topping

While whole potatoes are baking, prepare topping by combining ½ cup (125 mL) grated Cheddar cheese, 1 diced ripe avocado, ½ cup (125 mL) tomato salsa, 2 tbsp (25 mL) lime juice and 2 tbsp (25 mL) chopped fresh cilantro. Cut potatoes in half lengthwise and spoon topping over potatoes.

Baked Potatoes with Tuna Niçoise Topping

While whole potatoes are baking, prepare topping by combining one 6-oz (170 g) can drained and flaked water-packed tuna, 2 seeded and chopped plum tomatoes, 1 chopped anchovy fillet, 2 tbsp (25 mL) chopped black olives, 1 tsp (5 mL) chopped drained capers, 1 tbsp (15 mL) chopped fresh basil and ¼ tsp (1 mL) black pepper. Cut potatoes in half lengthwise and spoon topping over potatoes.

3	large baking potatoes	3
⅓ cup	sour cream or unflavored yogurt	75 mL
2 tbsp	olive oil or butter	25 mL
1½ cups	grated Gruyère or Cheddar cheese, divided	375 mL
¼ cup	chopped green onion or chives	50 mL
2 tsp	chopped fresh tarragon, or ½ tsp (2 mL) dried	10 mL
½ tsp	salt	2 mL
¼ tsp	black pepper	1 mL
½ cup	diced cooked bacon or ham	125 mL

1. Pierce potatoes with a fork. Place directly on rack and bake in preheated 400°F (200°C) toaster oven for 1 hour, or until potatoes are tender when pierced. Cool slightly.

2. Carefully cut potatoes in half lengthwise. Gently scoop out potato pulp, leaving enough shell to act as a container.

3. Place pulp in a large bowl and mash. Add sour cream, oil, ¾ cup (175 mL) cheese, green onion, tarragon, salt, pepper and bacon. Mix well.

4. Spoon mixture into potato shells, mounding in center. Sprinkle with remaining ¾ cup (175 mL) cheese.

5. Arrange potatoes on oven pan. Return to toaster oven and bake for 15 to 18 minutes, or until potatoes are heated through and cheese has melted.

Roasted Mini Potatoes

When my parents dug our large crop of new potatoes each year, the mini potatoes were not really prized as they were not considered good keepers. But my sister would pick out these little morsels and Mom would cook them just for her. Now mini potatoes have become a specialty at markets and food shops. Sizes vary, so adjust the baking time accordingly. For this recipe, 1-inch (2.5 cm) potatoes were used. The tiny potatoes are even more precious. If only larger potatoes are available, just cut them into 1-inch (2.5 cm) chunks.

MAKES 3 TO 4 SERVINGS

1½ lbs	mini potatoes	750 g
1 tbsp	olive oil	15 mL
½ tsp	dried oregano, sage or rosemary leaves	2 mL
½ tsp	salt	2 mL
¼ tsp	black pepper	1 mL
1 tbsp	lemon juice	15 mL

1. In a large bowl, toss potatoes with oil, oregano, salt and pepper. Spread potatoes on oven pan.

2. Bake in preheated 400°F (200°C) toaster oven for 35 to 40 minutes, shaking pan occasionally, until potatoes are golden and tender when pierced. Toss with lemon juice just before serving.

Sweet Potato Wedges
with Savory

Sweet potatoes have come a long way from the overly sweet casseroles that contained large amounts of brown sugar, butter, marshmallows and even maraschino cherries. Sweet and tender, these tubers can be roasted, baked, mashed, candied, boiled, broiled, grilled and even used in desserts. They are also often used in soups and stews.

Keep peeled sweet potatoes in water to prevent browning. (Drain well and pat dry before tossing with oil.) Their shelf life is shorter than that of regular potatoes, so try to use them within the week.

You can also use regular potatoes in this recipe, peeled or unpeeled. Bake them for 40 minutes, or until golden and tender when pierced.

MAKES 3 SERVINGS

1½ lbs	sweet potatoes (about 3 medium), peeled	750 g
2 tbsp	olive oil	25 mL
1 tbsp	cornmeal	15 mL
1 tsp	chopped fresh savory or thyme, or ½ tsp (2 mL) dried	5 mL
¾ tsp	salt	4 mL
½ tsp	black pepper	2 mL

1. Cut each sweet potato into 6 wedges and place in a large bowl. Add oil, cornmeal, savory, salt and pepper and toss. Spread potatoes on oven pan.

2. Bake in preheated 400°F (200°C) toaster oven for 35 minutes, or until potatoes test tender when pierced. Stir occasionally during cooking.

Potato Cake

This was a big hit in an Italian cooking class that I taught. It is hearty enough to be served as a meal along with a green salad or pepper salad (page 137). Use potatoes that mash well, such as Yukon Gold or baking potatoes. The potato cake also reheats well at 350°F (180°C) for 20 to 25 minutes, though it will be drier the second time.

For a vegetarian version, omit the ham and add 2 tbsp (25 mL) chopped oil-packed sun-dried tomatoes.

MAKES 4 TO 6 SERVINGS

Make Ahead

Cool potato mixture for 25 minutes before assembling pie. Once assembled, cover and refrigerate for up to a day. Add 8 to 10 minutes to baking time. Watch carefully to make sure top does not become too dark.

2 lbs	potatoes, peeled and cut in 2-inch (5 cm) pieces	1 kg
¼ cup	milk	50 mL
2 tbsp	butter or olive oil	25 mL
1 tsp	salt	5 mL
⅓ cup	grated Parmesan cheese	75 mL
2 tbsp	all-purpose flour	25 mL
2	eggs, beaten	2
¾ cup	grated Swiss cheese	175 mL
½ cup	diced ham or prosciutto	125 mL

Topping

¼ cup	fresh breadcrumbs	50 mL
2 tbsp	grated Parmesan cheese	25 mL
2 tbsp	melted butter or olive oil	25 mL

1. In a large saucepan, cook potatoes in boiling salted water until tender, about 20 to 25 minutes. Drain well and mash (you should have about 3½ cups/875 mL).
2. Add milk, butter, salt, Parmesan, flour and eggs to potatoes and stir in.
3. Spread half of mixture in a well-buttered 9-inch (23 cm) pie plate. Sprinkle Swiss cheese and ham over potato. Spread remaining potato mixture over cheese and ham.
4. For topping, in a small bowl, combine breadcrumbs, Parmesan and melted butter. Sprinkle over potato cake.
5. Bake in preheated 400°F (200°C) toaster oven for 35 minutes, or until top is crisp and golden. Let stand for 10 minutes before serving.

Grated Potato and Cheese Bake

This reminds me of a grated version of cheesy scalloped potatoes. For quick preparation, use the grating disc of the food processor, grating the potatoes just before assembling the dish. Use Yukon Gold or baking potatoes. Serve with cold roast chicken (page 72) and steamed broccoli.

MAKES 4 SERVINGS

Make Ahead

Cook onion mixture ahead and cool. Peel potatoes and cover with cold water. Drain potatoes, dry well and grate just before assembling dish.

2 tbsp	butter	25 mL
1	onion, chopped	1
1	stalk celery, chopped	1
2	cloves garlic, finely chopped	2
1 lb	potatoes, peeled and grated	500 g
1 cup	grated Cheddar cheese	250 mL
1¼ cups	milk, hot	300 mL
¾ tsp	salt	4 mL
¼ tsp	black pepper	1 mL
Pinch	ground nutmeg	Pinch

1. In a medium skillet, heat butter over medium heat. Add onion, celery and garlic. Cook, stirring occasionally, for 4 minutes, or until softened.

2. In a large bowl, combine cooked onion mixture with grated potatoes, cheese, hot milk, salt, pepper and nutmeg. Pour into a lightly greased 8-inch (2 L) square baking dish.

3. Bake in preheated 375°F (190°C) toaster oven for 45 to 50 minutes, or until potatoes test tender in center and are golden. Turn dish halfway through baking time. Let stand for 10 minutes before serving.

Hash Brown Gratin

A cozy make-ahead dish for the cottage or chalet. I like to serve this with cold roast beef and horseradish or cold roast pork and applesauce, though it goes well with fried eggs and chili sauce, too. Use leftover cooked potatoes or frozen hash brown potatoes.

MAKES 4 SERVINGS

Make Ahead

Assemble dish, cover and refrigerate for up to 4 hours, before baking.

2 tbsp	olive oil	25 mL
2	onions, chopped	2
2	cloves garlic, finely chopped	2
1 cup	fresh or frozen and defrosted corn kernels	250 mL
3 cups	diced cooked potatoes	750 mL
½ cup	sour cream	125 mL
3	green onions, chopped	3
2 tbsp	chopped fresh parsley	25 mL
¾ tsp	salt	4 mL
¼ tsp	black pepper	1 mL

Topping

½ cup	corn flakes cereal crumbs	125 mL
¼ cup	grated Cheddar cheese	50 mL

1. In a large skillet, heat oil over medium-high heat. Add onions, garlic and corn. Cook for 8 minutes, stirring occasionally, until onions and corn are lightly colored.

2. Remove skillet from heat. Stir in potatoes, sour cream, green onions, parsley, salt and pepper.

3. Spoon potatoes into a lightly greased 8-inch (2 L) square baking dish. Sprinkle with cereal crumbs and cheese.

4. Bake in preheated 350°F (180°C) toaster oven for 35 minutes, or until potatoes are hot and top is golden brown.

Butternut Squash and Fennel

Fennel, also called anise or finocchio, is a bulb with feathery greens. Left uncooked, it has a light licorice taste, and it is sometimes served raw with a tray of fruit in Italian homes and restaurants. When cooked, it becomes almost sweet. The fronds can be chopped to use as a garnish. When fennel is not available, celery is the usual substitute.

Toss any leftover baked squash and fennel with cooked rice or pasta, or add other roasted vegetables such as potatoes and red peppers.

MAKES 4 SERVINGS

1	butternut squash (about 1½ lbs/750 g)	1
1	onion, peeled and cut in 8 wedges	1
1	fennel bulb (about 1 lb/500 g), trimmed and sliced	1
2 tbsp	olive oil	25 mL
2 tbsp	water	25 mL
¾ tsp	salt	4 mL
¼ tsp	black pepper	1 mL
¼ tsp	dried oregano leaves	1 mL
3 tbsp	grated Parmesan cheese	45 mL

1. Peel squash and remove seeds. Cut squash into ½-inch (1 cm) pieces.

2. Place squash, onion and fennel in a 6-cup (1.5 L) casserole (with lid). Add oil, water, salt, pepper and oregano and stir.

3. Bake, covered, in preheated 425°F (220°C) toaster oven for 35 to 40 minutes, or until tender. (If pan becomes dry during cooking, add 2 tbsp/25 mL water.)

4. Remove cover and sprinkle vegetables with cheese. Bake, uncovered, for 10 to 12 minutes, or until slightly golden.

Rainbow Pepper Salad

Make this versatile salad in late summer when multi-colored peppers are overflowing at the market. Serve it with frittata (page 151), roast chicken (page 72) or tilapia (page 57), or toss with cooked pasta. You can also cut the peppers into smaller pieces to use as a topping for grilled bread or as a sandwich filling.

MAKES 4 TO 5 SERVINGS

3	bell peppers (red, yellow and orange), seeded and cut in 1-inch (2.5 cm) pieces	3
2 tbsp	olive oil	25 mL
1	onion, thinly sliced lengthwise	1
4	cloves garlic, peeled and cut in slivers	4
$\frac{1}{2}$ tsp	salt	2 mL
$\frac{1}{4}$ tsp	black pepper	1 mL
2 tbsp	balsamic vinegar	25 mL
2 tsp	drained capers	10 mL
2 tsp	chopped fresh oregano or basil, or $\frac{1}{2}$ tsp (2 mL) dried	10 mL
Pinch	granulated sugar	Pinch
2	anchovy fillets, chopped (optional)	2

1. In a large bowl, combine peppers, oil, onion, garlic, salt and pepper. Toss.
2. Turn peppers into a lightly greased 6-cup (1.5 L) baking dish.
3. Bake in preheated 400°F (200°C) toaster oven for 35 minutes, stirring twice during baking.
4. Remove peppers from oven and let cool for 15 minutes. Stir in vinegar, capers, oregano, sugar and anchovies, if using. Serve hot or at room temperature.

Ratatouille

Not a saucy ratatouille, this version is similar to a salad. It is excellent served hot, warm or at room temperature with lamb and fish, but it can also be used as a topping for baked potatoes (page 130) or grilled bread (page 46).

MAKES 4 SERVINGS

Variation

Ratatouille Antipasto
Cool ratatouille to room temperature. Toss with 2 seeded and chopped plum tomatoes, $\frac{1}{2}$ cup (125 mL) pitted black or green olives and 2 tbsp (25 mL) shredded fresh basil. Serve with crusty bread as an appetizer.

1	small eggplant (about 12 oz/375 g), cut in $\frac{1}{2}$-inch (1 cm) pieces	1
1	medium zucchini (about 8 oz/250 g), cut in $\frac{1}{2}$-inch (1 cm) pieces	1
$\frac{1}{2}$	red bell pepper, seeded and cut in $\frac{1}{2}$-inch (1 cm) pieces	$\frac{1}{2}$
1	onion, chopped	1
$\frac{1}{4}$ cup	olive oil	50 mL
$\frac{1}{2}$ tsp	herbes de Provence or dried thyme leaves	2 mL
$\frac{1}{2}$ tsp	salt	2 mL
$\frac{1}{4}$ tsp	black pepper	1 mL

1. In a large bowl, combine eggplant, zucchini, red pepper, onion, oil, herbes de Provence, salt and pepper. Spread over oven tray or shallow baking dish.
2. Bake in preheated 400°F (200°C) toaster oven for 35 to 40 minutes, or until tender and golden. Stir 3 times during baking.

Peperonata

This is another dish to make at the peak of pepper and tomato season, but with the availability of these vegetables year round, it also makes a colorful winter dish. Serve it with casseroles, meat, poultry, fish and egg dishes. If the peppers are long, cut them in half crosswise to make shorter strips.

The tomatoes can be left unpeeled, but the dish will look a bit nicer if they are peeled.

The peperonata can also be frozen. If it is very juicy when defrosted, just place in a saucepan and cook over medium-high heat for 10 to 15 minutes.

MAKES 4 TO 5 SERVINGS

2 tbsp	olive oil	25 mL
1	onion, thinly sliced	1
2	cloves garlic, peeled and thinly sliced	2
2	red bell peppers, seeded and thinly sliced	2
1	green bell pepper, seeded and thinly sliced	1
3	tomatoes, peeled, seeded and chopped	3
½ tsp	salt	2 mL
¼ tsp	granulated sugar	1 mL
¼ tsp	black pepper	1 mL
12	whole fresh basil leaves	12

1. In an 8-cup (2 L) casserole, combine oil, onion, garlic, red peppers, green pepper, tomatoes, salt, sugar, pepper and basil leaves.

2. Bake in preheated 400°F (200°C) toaster oven for 50 to 60 minutes, stirring several times, until peppers are soft and peperonata has thickened and is no longer watery. (Amount of liquid will depend on how juicy the tomatoes are.)

Peeling and Seeding Tomatoes

To peel tomatoes, remove cores and make a shallow X in blossom ends. Immerse tomatoes in boiling water for 30 seconds, then plunge into cold water. The skins will slip off easily. Cut tomatoes in half crosswise and gently squeeze or scrape out seeds.

Tomatoes Provençal

A timeless and easy tomato dish for a buffet, brunch or to add color to a dinner plate.
Choose tomatoes that are ripe and not too large.

MAKES 3 TO 6 SERVINGS

Make Ahead

Tomatoes can be assembled
up to 3 hours before baking.

3	tomatoes, halved crosswise	3
¾ cup	fresh breadcrumbs	175 mL
⅓ cup	chopped fresh parsley	75 mL
2	cloves garlic, minced	2
2 tbsp	chopped fresh basil	25 mL
¼ tsp	salt	1 mL
¼ tsp	black pepper	1 mL
2 tbsp	olive oil	25 mL

1. Gently remove seeds from tomatoes. Cut a thin piece from rounded end of tomato halves so they will sit flat. Place halves on lightly greased oven pan.

2. In a bowl, combine breadcrumbs, parsley, garlic, basil, salt, pepper and oil. Spread filling on tomatoes.

3. Bake in preheated 400°F (200°C) toaster oven for 20 minutes, or until tomatoes are just heated through. Do not overcook or tomatoes will collapse. (Fresh garden tomatoes may cook more quickly than storebought tomatoes out of season.)

Baked Asparagus with Parmesan

Baking asparagus is another way to serve this harbinger of spring. Select fat asparagus for this recipe and peel a few inches up the ends of the stalks if the skins are thick.

MAKES 3 SERVINGS

Make Ahead

After cooking asparagus in boiling water, plunge into cold water to cool and blot dry on a dish towel. Dish can be assembled up to 4 hours before baking.

Variation

Baked Fennel with Parmesan
Trim 2 medium bulbs fennel and cut each into 8 wedges. Cook in boiling water for 4 minutes. Bake for 20 to 25 minutes, or until tender.

1 lb	asparagus, tough ends removed and stems peeled at ends	500 g
2 tbsp	butter or olive oil	25 mL
2 tbsp	grated Parmesan cheese	25 mL

1. Bring a large skillet of salted water to a boil. Add asparagus and cook for 4 minutes. Drain well and blot dry on paper towels or a dish towel.
2. Arrange asparagus in an 8-inch (2 L) square baking dish. Dot with butter. Sprinkle with cheese.
3. Bake in preheated 375°F (190°C) toaster oven for 12 to 15 minutes, or until hot.

Cauliflower au Gratin

Along with learning to make a bed with hospital corners and the correct procedure for ironing a shirt, cauliflower with Cheddar cheese sauce was the first vegetable dish I learned to make when I took home ec in high school. Years later, during chef training, we made the same dish, but this time we used Gruyère. This can be served with a wedge of iceberg lettuce and sliced tomatoes.

MAKES 4 TO 6 SERVINGS

1	head cauliflower (about 3 lbs/1.5 kg), cut in florets	1
2 tbsp	butter	25 mL
1	onion, chopped	1
3 tbsp	all-purpose flour	45 mL
1½ cups	milk	375 mL
½ tsp	salt	2 mL
¼ tsp	black pepper	1 mL
Pinch	ground nutmeg	Pinch
1 cup	grated Cheddar or Gruyère cheese	250 mL
⅓ cup	fresh breadcrumbs	75 mL
⅓ cup	grated Parmesan cheese	75 mL

1. In a medium saucepan, bring a small amount of water to a boil. Add cauliflower, cover and cook for 4 minutes, or until just tender. Drain. Rinse under cold water and pat dry with tea towel.

2. Place cauliflower in a lightly greased 8-inch (2 L) square baking dish.

3. To prepare sauce, melt butter in a medium saucepan over medium heat. Add onion and cook, stirring occasionally, for 4 minutes, or until softened.

4. Add flour and cook, stirring, for 2 minutes. Whisk in milk. Bring to a boil and cook gently for 5 minutes, stirring occasionally. Remove from heat.

5. Stir in salt, pepper, nutmeg and Cheddar. Pour sauce over cauliflower.

6. Sprinkle breadcrumbs and Parmesan evenly over surface.

7. Bake in preheated 400°F (200°C) toaster oven for 15 to 20 minutes, or until top is golden and sauce is bubbling at edges.

Mashed Turnip Puff

A homey dish to accompany roast chicken, ham or cold meats. The sometimes sharp taste of turnip is softened with a touch of sugar, while the eggs and baking powder give it a lift.

MAKES 4 TO 5 SERVINGS

Make Ahead

Turnip can be cooked, mashed and refrigerated up to a day ahead.

1	turnip (about 2½ lbs/1.25 kg), peeled and cut in ½-inch (1 cm) pieces	1
2 tbsp	butter	25 mL
3 tbsp	all-purpose flour	45 mL
2	eggs, beaten	2
1 tbsp	pure maple syrup or packed brown sugar	15 mL
1 tsp	baking powder	5 mL
½ tsp	salt	2 mL

Topping

½ cup	fresh breadcrumbs	125 mL
2 tbsp	butter, melted	25 mL
½ tsp	paprika	2 mL

1. In a large saucepan, cook turnip in a large amount of boiling salted water for 35 minutes, or until tender. Drain well and mash. Cool for 15 minutes.
2. Add butter, flour, eggs, maple syrup, baking powder and salt to turnip. Combine thoroughly. Spoon into a lightly greased 6-cup (1.5 L) ovenproof serving dish.
3. In a small bowl, combine breadcrumbs, melted butter and paprika. Sprinkle over turnip.
4. Bake in preheated 350°F (180°C) toaster oven for 35 minutes, or until slightly puffed and set.

Corn and Red Peppers

Roasting brings out the sweetness of vegetables like corn and sweet peppers, and the combination adds color to a dinner plate. Use any leftovers in an omelet or frittata (page 151). Sometimes I stir leftovers into rice or couscous (page 59) or add them to a salad.

MAKES 3 TO 4 SERVINGS

(page 151). ... (page 59)

2 cups	fresh or frozen and defrosted corn kernels	500 mL
1	red bell pepper, seeded and chopped	1
1	onion, chopped	1
1	small jalapeño pepper, seeded and chopped	1
2 tbsp	olive oil	25 mL
½ tsp	ground cumin	2 mL
½ tsp	dried oregano leaves	2 mL
½ tsp	salt	2 mL
¼ tsp	black pepper	1 mL

Variation

Succotash
Add 1 cup (250 mL) cooked lima or edamame beans to corn mixture. (Edamame are fresh green soy beans, which must be shelled before eating. They are sold in the shell or shelled in the frozen section of supermarkets and occasionally fresh in markets.)

1. In a 6-cup (1.5 L) baking dish, combine corn, red pepper, onion, jalapeño, oil, cumin, oregano, salt and pepper.

2. Bake in preheated 400°F (200°C) toaster oven for 25 to 30 minutes, or until tender and golden. Stir 3 times during cooking.

Citrus Chicken with
Romesco Sauce (page 84)

Stuffed Pork Loin Roast with
Cranapple Sauce (page 107)

Old-fashioned Macaroni
and Cheese (page 116)

Spaghetti Pie (page 118)

Stuffed Baked Potatoes (page 130)

Monte Cristo Sandwiches (page 156)

Apple Snacking Muffins (page 174)

Peach Melba Cobbler (page 191)

Mushroom Rice Pilaf

Rice pilafs are such an easy dish to cook in the toaster oven, and once you have made a couple, you barely need a recipe. Just use twice as much liquid as rice. For a plain pilaf, omit the mushrooms. Once cooked, the pilaf will stay warm, covered, for at least 15 minutes.

MAKES 4 SERVINGS

Variation

Apricot Almond Rice Pilaf

Omit mushrooms. Add ⅓ cup (75 mL) diced dried apricots and ¼ cup (50 mL) toasted slivered almonds to saucepan with rice.

2 tbsp	butter	25 mL
1	onion, chopped	1
1 cup	sliced mushrooms	250 mL
1 cup	uncooked long-grain rice	250 mL
½ tsp	salt	2 mL
¼ tsp	black pepper	1 mL
¼ tsp	dried thyme leaves	1 mL
2 cups	chicken stock or vegetable stock	500 mL
2 tbsp	chopped fresh parsley	25 mL

1. In a large saucepan, melt butter over medium-high heat. Add onion and mushrooms. Cook, stirring occasionally, for 5 minutes, or until vegetables are softened.

2. Stir in rice, salt, pepper, thyme and stock. Bring to a boil. Transfer to a 6-cup (1.5 L) casserole (with lid).

3. Cook, covered, in preheated 350°F (180°C) toaster oven for 22 to 25 minutes, or until rice is tender and liquid is absorbed. Stir in parsley and fluff with a fork before serving.

Apple Stuffing Casserole

This teams well with pork tenderloin or cold roast turkey or chicken. You can also add ½ cup (125 mL) diced cooked bacon, ham or mortadella to the stuffing.

MAKES 4 SERVINGS

Make Ahead

Cool mixture before adding chicken stock. Transfer to baking dish, cover and refrigerate up to 4 hours before baking.

2 tbsp	butter	25 mL
1	onion, chopped	1
2	stalks celery, chopped	2
2	apples, peeled and chopped	2
4 cups	day-old bread cubes, lightly packed	1 L
¼ cup	dried cranberries	50 mL
¼ cup	chopped dried apricots	50 mL
1 cup	chicken stock or vegetable stock	250 mL
½ cup	apple juice	125 mL
2 tsp	dried sage leaves	10 mL
½ tsp	salt	2 mL
¼ tsp	black pepper	1 mL

1. In a large skillet, melt butter over medium heat. Add onion, celery and apples. Cook, stirring occasionally, for 5 minutes, or until apples are softened but not mushy. Place in a large bowl.

2. Add bread cubes, cranberries, apricots, stock, apple juice, sage, salt and pepper to bowl and combine. Transfer to a lightly greased 6-cup (1.5 L) baking dish.

3. Bake in preheated 350°F (180°C) toaster oven for 40 minutes, or until hot throughout and golden on top.

Breakfast and Brunch

Good Morning Grapefruit

A great way to start the day, especially on cool winter mornings. Use dark brown sugar if you have it.

MAKES 4 SERVINGS

2	large red or white grapefruit	2
⅓ cup	packed brown sugar	75 mL
¼ cup	slivered almonds	50 mL

1. Cut grapefruit in half crosswise. Remove center cores and section grapefruit using a serrated knife. Trim a small slice from bottom of each grapefruit half so they will not wobble.

2. Place grapefruit halves cut side up on oven tray. Sprinkle evenly with brown sugar and almonds.

3. Bake in preheated 400°F (200°C) toaster oven for 10 minutes, or until sugar melts and almonds are golden.

Breakfast Squares

This is a healthful alternative to muffins. Make them at least a day ahead for especially moist squares. Store them in a covered container and refrigerate for up to three days or freeze for up to three weeks. Cut into squares before freezing so you can defrost a few at a time.

MAKES 25 SQUARES

¼ cup	butter, melted	50 mL
½ cup	packed brown sugar	125 mL
2	eggs, beaten	2
1 cup	buttermilk or unflavored yogurt	250 mL
1 cup	all-purpose flour	250 mL
1 cup	rolled oats (not instant)	250 mL
½ cup	wheat bran or oat bran	125 mL
½ cup	dried cranberries	125 mL
½ cup	pitted chopped dates	125 mL
½ cup	chopped dried apricots	125 mL
¼ cup	flax seeds	50 mL
¼ cup	sunflower seeds	50 mL
2 tsp	baking soda	10 mL
½ tsp	ground cinnamon	2 mL

1. In a large bowl, combine melted butter, brown sugar, eggs and buttermilk.

2. In a separate bowl, combine flour, rolled oats, bran, cranberries, dates, apricots, flax seeds, sunflower seeds, baking soda and cinnamon. Add to egg mixture and combine well.

3. Pour into a lightly greased and parchment-lined 8-inch (2 L) square baking dish. Bake in preheated 350°F (180°C) toaster oven for 30 to 35 minutes, or until a toothpick inserted in center comes out clean. Cool and cut into squares.

Oatmeal Cinnamon French Toast

French toast, soft on the inside and crunchy on the outside, will entice even a non-morning person to the breakfast table. It also makes an easy supper on lazy days, served with sausages or ham, maple syrup or baked apples (page 195). Use egg bread or a soft bread that will absorb the liquid well.

MAKES 4 SLICES

3	eggs	3
½ cup	milk	125 mL
1 tbsp	granulated sugar	15 mL
½ tsp	vanilla	2 mL
Pinch	salt	Pinch
4	slices bread (about ¾ inch/2 cm thick)	4
¾ cup	rolled oats (not instant) or chopped pecans	175 mL
½ tsp	ground cinnamon	2 mL
3 tbsp	butter, melted	45 mL

1. In a large shallow dish, beat eggs. Add milk, sugar, vanilla and salt and beat together.

2. Add bread slices to egg mixture, turning gently to absorb liquid.

3. In another shallow dish, combine rolled oats and cinnamon. Dip soaked bread slices into oat mixture, turning to coat both sides.

4. Brush parchment-lined oven pan with half the melted butter. Place bread slices on pan in a single layer. Drizzle with remaining butter.

5. Bake in preheated 400°F (200°C) toaster oven for 10 minutes. Turn bread and bake for 10 minutes longer, or until slightly crisp and golden.

Spanish Potato Frittata

An adaptation of the Spanish potato omelet, this frittata is at home at breakfast, lunch or supper. If you wish, add ½ cup (125 mL) fresh or frozen and defrosted corn kernels to the egg mixture. Serve with chorizo sausage and sliced tomatoes. It is even good served cold.

MAKES 4 TO 6 SERVINGS

2 tbsp	olive oil, divided	25 mL
1	small Spanish onion, chopped	1
2	cloves garlic, finely chopped	2
6	eggs	6
3 cups	diced cooked potatoes (about 3 medium)	750 mL
¾ tsp	salt	4 mL
¼ tsp	paprika	1 mL
¼ tsp	black pepper	1 mL

1. In a skillet, heat 1 tbsp (15 mL) oil over medium-high heat. Add onion and garlic. Cook, stirring occasionally, until softened and slightly golden, about 4 minutes.

2. In a large bowl, beat eggs. Add onion mixture, potatoes, salt, paprika and pepper.

3. Brush a 9-inch (23 cm) pie plate (preferably nonstick) with remaining 1 tbsp (15 mL) olive oil. Pour in egg mixture.

4. Bake in preheated 350°F (180°C) toaster oven for 30 minutes, or until eggs are set. Let stand for 5 minutes before cutting into wedges.

Goat Cheese and Herb Soufflé

Soufflés really are easier than most people think. All they ask is that guests be seated when the soufflé comes out of the oven.

A 6-cup (1.5 L) soufflé dish is a handy dish for the toaster oven because of its convenient size and capacity. Use it for casseroles and gratins, too.

MAKES 3 TO 4 SERVINGS

Variations

Cheddar and Herb Soufflé
Replace goat cheese with 1 cup (250 mL) grated Cheddar cheese.

Goat Cheese and Spinach Soufflé
Add ½ cup (125 mL) chopped cooked spinach to sauce with goat cheese. (Squeeze spinach very dry before using.)

Goat Cheese and Asparagus Soufflé
Add ¾ cup (175 mL) chopped cooked asparagus or broccoli to sauce with goat cheese.

3 tbsp	butter	45 mL
3 tbsp	all-purpose flour	45 mL
1 cup	hot milk	250 mL
½ tsp	dry mustard	2 mL
¼ tsp	salt	1 mL
¼ tsp	black pepper	1 mL
4	eggs, separated	4
¾ cup	crumbled chèvre (goat cheese)	175 mL
2 tbsp	chopped fresh chives or green onion	25 mL
2 tsp	chopped fresh tarragon or savory, or ½ tsp (2 mL) dried	10 mL
¼ tsp	cream of tartar	1 mL

1. In a medium saucepan, melt butter over medium heat. Add flour and cook, stirring, for 3 minutes without browning.

2. Whisk in hot milk, mustard, salt and pepper. Cook, stirring constantly, for 2 minutes, or until sauce thickens. Remove from heat.

3. In a bowl, beat egg yolks. Stir ½ cup (125 mL) hot sauce into yolks. Add yolks back to sauce, return saucepan to heat and cook for 1 minute. Remove from heat and let sit for 10 minutes. Stir in goat cheese, chives and tarragon.

4. In a large, very clean bowl, beat egg whites with cream of tartar until stiff but not dry. Stir one-third of whites into cheese base. Then gently fold cheese mixture back into remaining whites.

5. Turn into a buttered 6-cup (1.5 L) soufflé dish or shallow gratin dish. Smooth surface.

6. Bake in preheated 350°F (180°C) toaster oven for 25 to 35 minutes, or until top is golden and firm and soufflé is slightly jiggly (cooking time will depend on size and shape of dish used).

Red Pepper Quiche

Cooked red pepper adds color and a surprisingly sweet flavor to many dishes. Chop the red pepper into small pieces so the quiche will slice cleanly. Serve with a tossed salad for brunch.

MAKES 4 TO 6 SERVINGS

Make Ahead

Pie shell can be prebaked up to 6 hours ahead. Keep at room temperature.

1	unbaked 9-inch (23 cm) pie shell, storebought or homemade (page 192)	1
2 tbsp	butter or olive oil	25 mL
1	red bell pepper, seeded and chopped	1
1	onion, chopped	1
1 cup	grated Gruyère cheese	250 mL
2	eggs	2
¾ cup	milk or sour cream	175 mL
¼ tsp	salt	1 mL
¼ tsp	black pepper	1 mL
2 tbsp	shredded fresh basil	25 mL

1. Line pastry shell with foil or parchment paper and fill with pie weights or dried beans, making sure foil or parchment paper does not hang over edges of plate. Bake in preheated 425°F (220°C) toaster oven for 15 to 18 minutes, or until pastry is golden brown around the edges. Remove pie weights, return pastry to oven and continue to bake crust for 5 to 7 minutes, or until raw appearance is gone.

2. Meanwhile, in a large skillet, melt butter over medium heat. Add red pepper and onion and cook, stirring occasionally, for about 10 minutes, or until softened and moisture has evaporated. Cool slightly.

3. Sprinkle cheese over prebaked pie shell. Spoon pepper mixture over cheese.

4. In a medium bowl, beat eggs. Blend in milk, salt and pepper. Carefully pour eggs over pepper mixture. Sprinkle basil over top.

5. Bake in preheated 350°F (180°C) toaster oven for 45 minutes, or until center is set. If necessary, turn dish halfway through baking time for more even cooking. Let stand for 10 minutes before serving.

Apple Noodle Casserole

This is similar to a noodle kugel. A popular brunch dish served with sausages, it also goes well with roast chicken (page 72) and a grated carrot salad.

MAKES 4 TO 6 SERVINGS

8 oz	uncooked extra-broad egg noodles	250 g
4	eggs	4
¼ cup	butter, melted	50 mL
1½ cups	storebought or homemade applesauce	375 mL
½ cup	orange juice concentrate	125 mL
¼ cup	packed brown sugar	50 mL
¼ cup	golden raisins or dried cranberries	50 mL
1 tsp	vanilla	5 mL
¼ tsp	ground cinnamon	1 mL

1. Cook noodles in a large amount of boiling salted water until just tender, about 8 minutes. Drain well.

2. In a large bowl, beat eggs. Add cooked noodles, melted butter, applesauce, orange juice concentrate, brown sugar, raisins, vanilla and cinnamon. Mix well. Turn into a lightly greased 8-inch (2 L) baking dish.

3. Bake in preheated 350°F (180°C) toaster oven for 35 to 40 minutes, or until set in center. Let stand for up to 20 minutes before serving.

Mushroom Bread Cups

Creamy mushrooms baked in bread cups make an attractive side dish for bacon and eggs, but these can also be served as a starter. The "cream" is actually cheese that melts during baking.

MAKES 6 SERVINGS

Make Ahead

Toast cups can be prepared up to 4 hours ahead and left at room temperature. Mushrooms can be cooked ahead and left at room temperature for an hour before assembling.

6	slices white or whole wheat sandwich bread, crusts removed	6
2 tbsp	olive oil, divided	25 mL
2 cups	sliced mushrooms (about 8 oz/250 g)	500 mL
1	clove garlic, finely chopped	1
3	green onions, chopped	3
¼ tsp	salt	1 mL
¼ tsp	black pepper	1 mL
⅔ cup	crumbled chèvre (goat cheese)	150 mL

1. Flatten bread slices with a rolling pin. Fit into six lightly greased muffin cups. Brush with 1 tbsp (15 mL) olive oil. Bake in preheated 350°F (180°C) toaster oven for 5 minutes. Remove from oven.

2. Meanwhile, in a large skillet, heat remaining 1 tbsp (15 mL) oil over medium-high heat. Add mushrooms and garlic. Cook, stirring occasionally, for 6 to 8 minutes, or until moisture has evaporated. Cool for 15 minutes. Stir in green onions, salt and pepper.

3. Place half of cheese in bottom of bread cups. Divide mushroom mixture evenly over cheese. Top with remaining cheese.

4. Return to oven and continue to bake for 20 minutes, or until edges of bread are golden and cheese has melted.

Monte Cristo Sandwiches

This sandwich is a combination of French toast (because the sandwich is dipped in egg and milk) and a grilled ham and cheese. Lightly butter the bread before assembling the sandwiches if you wish.

MAKES 2 SANDWICHES

4	slices multigrain or brown bread	4
1 tbsp	Russian-style mustard	15 mL
4	thin slices Swiss cheese	4
2	slices Black Forest ham	2
2	eggs	2
1/4 cup	milk	50 mL
1/4 tsp	salt	1 mL
1/4 tsp	black pepper	1 mL
1 tbsp	olive oil or melted butter, divided	15 mL

1. Place 2 slices of bread on a flat surface. Spread with mustard. Top each with a slice of cheese, a slice of ham and another slice of cheese. Top with remaining bread slices.

2. In a shallow dish, beat together eggs. Beat in milk, salt and pepper.

3. Carefully dip both sides of sandwiches into egg mixture.

4. Brush parchment-lined oven pan with $1\frac{1}{2}$ tsp (7 mL) olive oil. Place sandwiches on pan.

5. Bake in preheated 400°F (200°C) toaster oven for 10 minutes. Carefully flip sandwiches and brush with remaining $1\frac{1}{2}$ tsp (7 mL) oil. Cook for 8 to 10 minutes longer, or until golden and slightly crispy.

Chicken Turnovers

Frozen prepared puff pastry is so easy to use. Only half a package is needed for this recipe, so keep the remaining pastry frozen or use any defrosted within two days. These turnovers are basically a chicken salad tucked into puff pastry, but they look as if you have really been cooking.

You can also use cooked turkey or ham in these turnovers. For a vegetarian version, in place of chicken, use canned black beans that have been rinsed and well drained.

MAKES 4 TURNOVERS

Make Ahead

Turnovers can be assembled up to 6 hours earlier, covered well and refrigerated until baking time. Brush with glaze just before baking.

1 cup	diced cooked chicken	250 mL
½ cup	chopped celery	125 mL
1	green onion, chopped	1
¼ cup	mayonnaise	50 mL
1 tbsp	mango chutney	15 mL
¼ tsp	curry powder	1 mL
¼ tsp	salt	1 mL
½	14-oz (397 g) package frozen puff pastry, defrosted but cold	½
1	egg	1
1 tbsp	milk	15 mL

1. In a bowl, combine chicken, celery, green onion, mayonnaise, chutney, curry powder and salt.

2. On a lightly floured surface, roll pastry into a 10-inch (25 cm) square. Cut into 4 squares. Place one-quarter of filling in center of each square.

3. In a small bowl or measuring cup, beat together egg and milk. Brush edges of pastry with egg mixture.

4. Fold each pastry in half diagonally to encase filling, pressing to seal tightly. Place turnovers on ungreased oven pan and brush with egg mixture.

5. Place pan on inverted bottom rack and bake in preheated 375°F (190°C) toaster oven for 25 to 28 minutes, or until pastry is puffed, golden and flaky.

Baked Sausages and Apples

A simple yet hearty brunch dish to serve on frosty days. Or serve for dinner along with baked beans, coleslaw (page 95) and homemade bread. Turkey sausages or other sausages can be substituted for Italian sausages.

MAKES 4 SERVINGS

1 lb	mild or hot Italian sausages	500 g
2	apples, peeled and cut in thick slices	2
1	onion, peeled and thinly sliced	1
½ cup	apple juice	125 mL
½ tsp	Dijon mustard	2 mL
½ tsp	dried sage leaves	2 mL

1. Cut each sausage into 3 pieces. Place in an 8-inch (2 L) baking dish. Add apple slices, onion, apple juice, mustard and sage. Stir to combine.

2. Bake in preheated 375°F (190°C) toaster oven for 40 to 45 minutes, or until sausages are cooked and golden and apples are tender. Stir gently 3 times during cooking.

Country Ham Loaf

When you have lots of leftover baked ham and you can't face another ham sandwich, transform the trimmings into a baked ham loaf. Serve warm or cold with eggs or home fries.

   Chop the ham finely in a food processor using on/off pulses (if the ham is too coarsely chopped, the loaf tends to fall apart).

MAKES 4 TO 5 SERVINGS

3 cups	minced cooked ham (about 1 lb/500 g)	750 mL
1 cup	fresh breadcrumbs	250 mL
2	eggs, beaten	2
1/2 cup	milk or pineapple juice	125 mL
2 tsp	Russian-style mustard	10 mL
1 tsp	Worcestershire sauce	5 mL
1/4 tsp	black pepper	1 mL
Glaze		
1/4 cup	maple syrup	50 mL
2 tbsp	packed brown sugar	25 mL
2 tbsp	lemon juice	25 mL
Pinch	ground cloves	Pinch

1. In a large bowl, combine ham, breadcrumbs, eggs, milk, mustard, Worcestershire and pepper. Pack into a parchment-lined 8- by 4-inch (1.5 L) loaf pan, making sure paper does not extend beyond edges of pan. Smooth surface.

2. Bake in preheated 375°F (190°C) toaster oven for 30 minutes.

3. Meanwhile, in a small bowl, combine maple syrup, brown sugar, lemon juice and cloves. Spoon over loaf and continue to bake for 30 to 35 minutes, or until top is golden and glaze has disappeared down sides of pan. Let stand in pan for 10 minutes before unmolding.

Corned Beef Hash

Some of the greatest restaurants serve hash, often as a brunch or lunch dish. To many hash lovers, it brings back memories of Mom's home cooking. The dish was probably never the same twice as it depended on what was left over, which may be why hash has a bad name. Most often it is cooked on the stove top with additions such as mushrooms, celery, green peppers and even olives, but it browns up perfectly when cooked in the toaster oven.

This version is Irish influenced, using cabbage. Buy corned beef at the deli counter, or you can use cubed ham, chicken or turkey. Serve with chili sauce, pickled beets or ketchup.

MAKE 3 SERVINGS

2 tbsp	butter	25 mL
1	onion, chopped	1
2 cups	chopped cabbage	500 mL
½	red bell pepper, seeded and chopped	½
3	eggs, beaten	3
4 cups	cubed cooked potatoes	1 L
2 cups	cubed cooked corned beef (about 10 oz/300 g)	500 mL
2 tbsp	chopped fresh parsley	25 mL
2	green onions, chopped	2
½ tsp	salt	2 mL
¼ tsp	black pepper	1 mL

1. In a large skillet, heat butter over medium heat. Add onion, cabbage and red pepper. Cook, stirring occasionally, for 6 minutes, or until vegetables are softened.

2. In a large bowl, beat eggs. Add cabbage mixture, potatoes, corned beef, parsley, green onions, salt and pepper and combine. Spoon into a lightly greased 8-inch (2 L) square baking dish.

3. Bake in preheated 375°F (190°C) toaster oven for 30 minutes, or until top is crispy.

Breads, Muffins, Cookies and Bars

Banana Bread

Banana bread seems to taste better when it is made a day ahead. This loaf will also keep, well wrapped and refrigerated, for up to three days, or it can be frozen for up to a month. Serve it sliced with softened cream cheese, yogurt cheese (page 189) or sweet (unsalted) butter.

MAKES ONE 8- BY 4-INCH (1.5 L) LOAF

Variation

Banana Orange Bread
Add 1 tbsp (15 mL) grated orange zest to wet ingredients.

2 cups	all-purpose flour	500 mL
1 tsp	baking powder	5 mL
1 tsp	baking soda	5 mL
1/4 tsp	salt	1 mL
1/2 cup	butter, melted	125 mL
1/2 cup	packed brown sugar	125 mL
2	eggs	2
1 1/2 cups	mashed ripe banana (about 3 bananas)	375 mL
1/3 cup	milk	75 mL
1 tsp	vanilla	5 mL

1. In a large bowl, combine flour, baking powder, baking soda and salt.

2. In a separate bowl, stir together melted butter and brown sugar. Beat in eggs one at a time. Stir in banana, milk and vanilla.

3. Pour wet ingredients into dry ingredients and mix just until combined. Scrape into a greased and parchment-lined 8- by 4-inch (1.5 L) loaf pan.

4. Bake in preheated 350°F (180°C) toaster oven for 60 to 65 minutes, or until a cake tester inserted in center comes out clean. Turn oven pan halfway through baking time. Let stand in pan for 10 minutes before turning out onto rack.

Citrus Tea Bread

Simple and fresh tasting, this tea bread can be served plain or with fresh or stewed fruit. The bread freezes well, so serve half now, wrap the remaining and freeze for up to a month.

MAKES ONE 8- BY 4-INCH (1.5 L) LOAF

Variation

Citrus Herb Bread
Add 2 tsp (10 mL) chopped fresh thyme, rosemary, lemon verbena or lavender flowers to batter with grated citrus zest.

½ cup	butter, softened	125 mL
¾ cup	granulated sugar	175 mL
2	eggs	2
1 tbsp	grated lemon zest	15 mL
1 tbsp	grated orange zest	15 mL
1⅓ cups	all-purpose flour	325 mL
1 tsp	baking powder	5 mL
¼ tsp	salt	1 mL
½ cup	milk	125 mL
⅓ cup	confectioner's (icing) sugar	75 mL
⅓ cup	orange juice	75 mL
¼ cup	lemon juice	50 mL

1. In a large bowl, cream together butter and sugar until light. Beat in eggs one at a time. Stir in lemon zest and orange zest.

2. In a separate bowl, combine flour, baking powder and salt. Add to butter mixture alternately with milk, making three liquid and two dry additions. Spoon into a greased and parchment-lined 8- by 4-inch (1.5 L) loaf pan.

3. Bake in preheated 350°F (180°C) toaster oven for about 55 minutes, or until a cake tester inserted in center comes out clean.

4. Meanwhile, in a measuring cup, combine confectioner's sugar, orange juice and lemon juice. Stir to dissolve sugar.

5. Using a skewer, pierce baked loaf in several places. Gradually spoon glaze over loaf. Cool loaf for 15 minutes before removing from pan. Cool completely on rack.

Farmhouse Seed Bread

I named this when I was looking for a rustic-sounding name for a bread I used to take to market. It was a great seller. Ideal for sandwiches and toast, I still get requests for it.

This bread freezes very well. Slice it, wrap in freezer bags and defrost as needed.

MAKES 2 LOAVES

1¼ cups	lukewarm water, divided	300 mL
2 tbsp	honey	25 mL
1 tbsp	active dry yeast (1 package)	15 mL
2 tbsp	fancy molasses	25 mL
2 tbsp	vegetable oil	25 mL
¼ cup	sunflower seeds	50 mL
¼ cup	flax seeds	50 mL
2 tbsp	poppy seeds	25 mL
2 tbsp	sesame seeds	25 mL
1 tsp	salt	5 mL
1 cup	whole wheat flour	250 mL
2 cups	all-purpose flour, approx.	500 mL

1. In a large bowl, combine ½ cup (125 mL) warm water, honey and yeast. Stir and let rest for 8 minutes, or until yeast becomes bubbly.

2. Add remaining ¾ cup (175 mL) warm water, molasses, oil, sunflower seeds, flax seeds, poppy seeds, sesame seeds and salt.

3. Stir in whole wheat flour and 1 cup (250 mL) all-purpose flour to form a wet dough. Add more all-purpose flour until dough is too stiff to stir, then turn out onto a floured surface. Knead for 8 minutes, adding enough flour to make a pliable dough.

4. Place dough in a lightly oiled bowl, turning dough to coat with oil. Cover bowl with plastic wrap. Let rise in a warm place until doubled in bulk, about 1 hour.

5. Deflate dough. Divide into two pieces. Shape into oval loaves about 8 inches (20 cm) long. Place seam side down on lightly greased oven pan.

6. Cut three diagonal slashes in top of each loaf. Dust lightly with flour. Let rise for 35 to 40 minutes, or until doubled in volume. (Loaves will grow together.)

7. Bake on inverted bottom rack in preheated 375°F (190°C) toaster oven for 30 to 35 minutes, or until loaves are golden brown and sound hollow when removed from pan and tapped on bottoms. Turn oven pan halfway through baking time. Cool completely on rack.

Working with Yeast

Dry yeast is available in both packages and cans. The recipes in this book use packaged active dry "traditional" yeast. Check the expiry date to make sure the yeast is fresh. When working with yeast, the warm water or milk should be about 110°F (45°C). If the liquid is too hot, the yeast may be killed. If the liquid is cooler, the yeast will still work; it will just take longer.

Dry yeast is activated by the addition of liquid and sugar, and it should bubble or foam. If nothing happens, the yeast may be out of date, and you'll need to buy fresh.

Raisin and Rosemary
Soda Bread

Ireland's most popular bread bakes perfectly in the toaster oven, without heating up the whole kitchen. For a plain soda bread, omit the rosemary and raisins.

This loaf has a longer shape than the traditional round loaf.

MAKES ONE 9-INCH (23 CM) LOAF

Variations

Cheddar and Sun-dried Tomato Bread
Omit rosemary and raisins. Add 1 cup (250 mL) grated Cheddar cheese and 3 tbsp (45 mL) chopped dry or oil-packed sun-dried tomatoes.

Apricot Caraway Soda Bread
Omit rosemary and raisins. Add ¾ cup (175 mL) diced dried apricots and 2 tsp (10 mL) caraway seeds.

2½ cups	all-purpose flour	625 mL
½ cup	whole wheat flour	125 mL
1 tsp	salt	5 mL
1 tsp	baking soda	5 mL
1 tbsp	chopped fresh rosemary, or 1½ tsp (7 mL) dried	15 mL
1 cup	raisins (preferably golden)	250 mL
1¾ cups	buttermilk or unflavored yogurt	425 mL

1. In a large bowl, combine all-purpose flour, whole wheat flour, salt, baking soda, rosemary and raisins. Combine thoroughly.

2. Add buttermilk. Stir to combine but do not overmix (dough will be slightly sticky). Turn onto a floured surface.

3. With floured hands, shape dough into a loaf about 9 inches (23 cm) long. Cut 5 diagonal slashes in top. Place on lightly floured oven pan.

4. Place on inverted bottom rack and bake in preheated 400°F (200°C) toaster oven for 20 minutes. Reduce heat to 350°F (180°C) and continue to bake for 20 minutes, or until bread sounds hollow when tapped on bottom. Turn oven pan halfway through baking time. Cool on rack.

Cornbread

Cornbreads can range in texture from firm to pudding-like. This one is a combination, and it can be served as a side dish or in place of bread. Although it can be wrapped well and frozen, it is best served the day it is made.

MAKES ABOUT 9 LARGE PIECES

1 cup	all-purpose flour	250 mL
¾ cup	cornmeal	175 mL
2 tbsp	granulated sugar	25 mL
2 tsp	baking soda	10 mL
½ tsp	salt	2 mL
2	eggs	2
1 cup	buttermilk or unflavored yogurt	250 mL
¼ cup	olive oil	50 mL
1 cup	fresh or frozen and defrosted corn kernels	250 mL
1	4-oz (114 mL) can chopped green chilies	1
1 cup	grated Cheddar cheese	250 mL

1. In a large bowl, combine flour, cornmeal, sugar, baking soda and salt.
2. In a separate bowl, beat eggs until combined. Stir in buttermilk, oil, corn, chilies and cheese.
3. Add wet ingredients to dry ingredients and stir just to combine. Scrape into a lightly greased and parchment-lined 8-inch (2 L) square baking dish.
4. Bake in preheated 375°F (190°C) toaster oven for 30 minutes, or until a cake tester inserted in center comes out clean. Serve hot or warm.

Garlic Cheese Bread

A perfect accompaniment for many dishes, from pasta to a simple green salad. You can double the recipe and cook a second batch while the first batch is being served.

MAKES 4 SLICES

Make Ahead

Bread can be spread with garlic butter and refrigerated, covered, for up to 6 hours.

¼ cup	butter, softened	50 mL
2	cloves garlic, minced	2
2 tbsp	chopped fresh parsley	25 mL
4	slices French or Italian bread, about ¾ inch (2 cm) thick	4
½ cup	grated Cheddar or Fontina cheese	125 mL

1. In a small bowl, cream together butter, garlic and parsley. Spread over bread slices.
2. Place bread on oven pan. Broil under preheated toaster oven broiler for 3 to 4 minutes, or until starting to sizzle.
3. Sprinkle cheese over bread. Continue to broil for 1 to 2 minutes, or until cheese melts and edges are golden. Let stand for 1 to 2 minutes, then cut into smaller pieces.

Dinner Rolls

The toaster oven bakes rolls to a lovely golden brown. Any extra rolls can be broken apart, wrapped separately and frozen.

MAKES 8 ROLLS

Variations

Whole Wheat Rolls
Replace 1 cup (250 mL) all-purpose flour with whole wheat flour.

Cheddar Rolls
Add ¾ cup (175 mL) grated Cheddar cheese with first addition of flour.

Cinnamon Raisin Rolls
Add ½ tsp (2 mL) ground cinnamon to first flour addition. Knead in ¾ cup (175 mL) raisins while kneading in last amount of flour.

½ cup	warm water	125 mL
1 tsp	granulated sugar	5 mL
1 tbsp	active dry yeast (1 package)	15 mL
¾ cup	warm milk	175 mL
2 tbsp	honey	25 mL
2 tbsp	melted butter or vegetable oil	25 mL
1 tsp	salt	5 mL
3 cups	all-purpose flour, approx.	750 mL

1. In a large bowl, combine water, sugar and yeast. Stir and let rest for 8 minutes, or until yeast becomes bubbly.

2. Add warm milk, honey, melted butter, salt and 2 cups (500 mL) flour to yeast mixture. Stir to combine and form a wet dough.

3. Continue to add flour until dough is too stiff to stir, then turn out onto a floured surface. Knead dough for 8 minutes, adding enough flour to make a soft, pliable dough.

4. Place dough in a lightly oiled bowl, turning to coat dough with oil. Cover bowl with plastic wrap. Let rise in a warm place until doubled in bulk, about 1 hour.

5. Deflate dough. Divide into 8 equal portions and shape into rolls.

6. Arrange rolls in a lightly greased deep 9-inch (23 cm) round cake pan. Dust surface lightly with flour. Let rise until doubled in bulk, about 35 to 40 minutes.

7. Bake in preheated 375°F (190°C) toaster oven for 25 minutes, or until bottoms sound hollow when rolls are removed from pan. Turn oven pan halfway through baking time. Remove rolls from pan and cool on rack.

Old-fashioned Tea Biscuits

Light tender tea biscuits were once the pillar of a good cook's reputation. Often served as a bread substitute, they were also used as the base in fruit shortcakes.

Tea biscuits and scones (the names are often used interchangeably) are best served the day they are baked, although they can also be wrapped well and frozen. When I was working in Australia, rock buns became my favorite variation of these; they were filled with fruit and served with cheese.

MAKES 8 TO 9 BISCUITS

Variations

Cheese Biscuits
Add ¾ cup (175 mL) grated Cheddar cheese to flour mixture after cutting in butter and shortening.

Rock Buns
Add ½ cup (125 mL) dried fruit to dry ingredients (e.g., currants, cranberries, blueberries, raisins or diced apricots).

1½ cups	all-purpose flour	375 mL
2 tbsp	granulated sugar	25 mL
2 tsp	baking powder	10 mL
½ tsp	salt	2 mL
¼ cup	butter, cold, cut in pieces	50 mL
¼ cup	shortening, cold, cut in pieces	50 mL
⅓ cup	milk	75 mL
1	egg	1

1. In a large bowl, combine flour, sugar, baking powder and salt.
2. Using a pastry blender or two knives, cut in butter and shortening until mixture is in tiny bits.
3. In a small bowl or measuring cup, combine milk and egg. Stir most of liquid into dry ingredients with a fork. Add more liquid as necessary, until a soft dough forms.
4. Turn dough out onto a lightly floured surface and knead four or five times until dough comes together. Pat dough to ¾-inch (2 cm) thickness.
5. Using a floured 2-inch (5 cm) cookie cutter, cut dough into 5 or 6 rounds. Reshape remaining dough and cut into rounds. Place on ungreased oven pan.
6. Bake on inverted lower rack in preheated 400°F (200°C) toaster oven for 12 to 14 minutes, or until biscuits are golden brown. Cool on a wire rack.

Banana Oatmeal Muffins

Although muffins can be frozen, they are always best when freshly baked. The toaster oven is perfect for making small batches.

When bananas are beyond their best for eating, muffins or banana bread (page 162) are the perfect solution (slightly overripe bananas can be frozen for up to three weeks; defrost, peel and mash before using). Children may not eat brown bananas, but they will devour these muffins, especially if they contain chocolate chips.

MAKES 6 MUFFINS

Variation

Banana Chocolate Chip Muffins
Add ½ cup (125 mL) chocolate chips to dry ingredients.

1 cup	all-purpose flour	250 mL
½ cup	rolled oats (not instant)	125 mL
⅓ cup	packed brown sugar	75 mL
¾ tsp	baking powder	4 mL
½ tsp	baking soda	2 mL
½ tsp	ground cinnamon	2 mL
¼ tsp	salt	1 mL
1	egg	1
½ cup	mashed ripe banana (about 1 banana)	125 mL
½ cup	buttermilk	125 mL
¼ cup	vegetable oil	50 mL
½ tsp	vanilla	2 mL

Topping

2 tbsp	packed brown sugar	25 mL
1 tbsp	rolled oats (not instant)	15 mL

1. In a large bowl, combine flour, rolled oats, brown sugar, baking powder, baking soda, cinnamon and salt.

2. In a separate bowl, beat egg. Stir in mashed banana, buttermilk, oil and vanilla.

3. Add wet ingredients to dry ingredients. Stir just to combine. Spoon batter into six lightly greased muffin cups.

4. For topping, in a small bowl, combine brown sugar and rolled oats. Sprinkle topping over muffins.

5. Bake in preheated 400°F (200°C) toaster oven for 18 to 20 minutes, or until tops of muffins spring back when lightly touched in center. Turn pan halfway through cooking time. Cool muffins in pan for 5 minutes before turning out onto a rack.

Lemon Ginger Fruit Muffins

Serve this muffin as a tea-time treat with fresh fruit. Choose fresh or frozen fruit such as blueberries, raspberries, cranberries and red currants. If you are using frozen fruit, do not defrost before adding it to the batter.

MAKES 6 MUFFINS

1½ cups	all-purpose flour	375 mL
½ cup	granulated sugar	125 mL
2 tbsp	chopped candied ginger	25 mL
1 tsp	baking powder	5 mL
½ tsp	ground ginger	2 mL
¼ tsp	salt	1 mL
1	egg	1
¾ cup	milk	175 mL
¼ cup	butter, melted	50 mL
1 tbsp	grated lemon zest	15 mL
½ cup	fresh or frozen berries	125 mL
2 tbsp	confectioner's (icing) sugar	25 mL
1 tsp	lemon juice	5 mL

1. In a large bowl, combine flour, granulated sugar, candied ginger, baking powder, ground ginger and salt.

2. In a separate bowl, beat egg. Stir in milk, melted butter and lemon zest. Add to dry ingredients with berries. Stir just until combined.

3. Spoon batter into six lightly greased muffin cups. Bake in preheated 375°F (190°C) toaster oven for 20 to 22 minutes, or until tops of muffins spring back when lightly touched. Turn pan halfway through baking time. Cool muffins in pan for 5 minutes before turning out onto a rack.

4. Meanwhile, in a small bowl or measuring cup, combine confectioner's sugar and lemon juice. Brush or spoon syrup over muffin tops while muffins are still warm.

Date Orange Muffins

Serve these delicious lactose-free muffins for a light but nutritious start to the day. For a more wholesome muffin, substitute ½ cup (125 mL) whole wheat flour for ½ cup (125 mL) all-purpose flour.

MAKES 6 MUFFINS

1⅓ cups	all-purpose flour	325 mL
⅓ cup	packed brown sugar	75 mL
1 tsp	baking powder	5 mL
½ tsp	baking soda	2 mL
¼ tsp	salt	1 mL
½ cup	chopped pitted dates	125 mL
1	egg	1
1 tbsp	grated orange zest	15 mL
¾ cup	orange juice	175 mL
¼ cup	vegetable oil	50 mL
½ tsp	vanilla	2 mL

1. In a large bowl, combine flour, brown sugar, baking powder, baking soda, salt and dates.

2. In a separate bowl, beat egg. Beat in orange zest, orange juice, oil and vanilla. Add to dry ingredients and stir just to combine.

3. Spoon batter into six lightly greased muffin cups. Bake in preheated 375°F (190°C) toaster oven for 22 minutes, or until muffin tops are firm to the touch and golden. Turn pan halfway through baking time. Cool muffins in pan for 5 minutes before turning out onto a rack.

Apple Snacking Muffins

The aroma of these cake-like muffins wafting through the house will attract the attention of adults and children alike. Serve as a breakfast, snack or lunchbox item. Applesauce makes these muffins nice and moist; serve any extra alongside the baked muffins.

For nicely rounded tops, use an ice-cream scoop to fill the muffin cups.

MAKES 6 MUFFINS

1 cup	all-purpose flour	250 mL
½ cup	rolled oats (not instant)	125 mL
⅓ cup	packed brown sugar	75 mL
2 tsp	baking powder	10 mL
¾ tsp	ground cinnamon	4 mL
¼ tsp	salt	1 mL
Pinch	ground cloves	Pinch
1	egg	1
¼ cup	butter, melted	50 mL
¾ cup	sweetened or unsweetened applesauce	175 mL
1	apple, peeled and grated	1
1 tsp	vanilla	5 mL

Topping

2 tsp	granulated sugar	10 mL
¼ tsp	ground cinnamon	1 mL

1. In a large bowl, combine flour, rolled oats, brown sugar, baking powder, cinnamon, salt and cloves.

2. In a separate bowl, beat egg. Stir in butter, applesauce, grated apple and vanilla. Add to dry ingredients. Stir just to combine. Spoon batter into six lightly greased muffin cups.

3. For topping, in a small bowl, combine granulated sugar and cinnamon. Sprinkle over muffin tops.

4. Bake in preheated 400°F (200°C) toaster oven for 20 minutes, or until tops are firm to the touch. Turn pan halfway through baking time. Cool muffins in pan for 5 minutes before turning out onto a rack.

Peanut Butter Chocolate Chip Cookies

Make a batch of cookie dough and bake a few at a time in the toaster oven so they are always fresh. The dough for this cookie-jar favorite can be kept in the refrigerator for up to three days, or it can be frozen. Defrost in the refrigerator before using.

You can omit the chocolate for plain peanut butter cookies.

**MAKES ABOUT
22 COOKIES**

¼ cup	butter, softened	50 mL
¼ cup	granulated sugar	50 mL
¼ cup	packed brown sugar	50 mL
1	egg, beaten	1
⅓ cup	peanut butter	75 mL
¾ cup	all-purpose flour	175 mL
¼ tsp	baking soda	1 mL
Pinch	salt	Pinch
½ cup	chopped semisweet or white chocolate, or chocolate chips	125 mL

1. In a large bowl, beat together butter and both sugars until light. Add egg and peanut butter and beat until light.

2. In a separate bowl, combine flour, baking soda, salt and chocolate. Add to peanut butter mixture. Stir until ingredients are well mixed.

3. Drop 8 mounds of dough in 1 tbsp (15 mL) measures onto lightly greased oven pan. Flatten slightly with back of a fork dipped in granulated sugar.

4. Bake on inverted bottom rack in preheated 375°F (190°C) toaster oven for about 10 minutes, or until golden brown. Turn pan halfway through baking time. Let cool on pan for 5 minutes before transferring to a rack. Refrigerate or freeze remaining dough or continue to bake batches until all dough is used.

Macadamia Nut Cookies

These shortbread-like cookies are embellished with macadamia nuts. Serve at tea time or for dessert with a fresh fruit salad that contains pineapple and/or mango. Most macadamia nuts are salted. Personally, I don't mind using them this way, but if you prefer unsalted, rinse the nuts and dry well before using. Rice flour is often used for shortbread and it makes these cookies nice and tender. Look for it in the baking section.

Refrigerate or freeze this dough and bake single batches of cookies as you need them.

**MAKES ABOUT
24 COOKIES**

½ cup	butter, softened	125 mL
½ cup	packed brown sugar	125 mL
1	egg, beaten	1
¼ tsp	vanilla	1 mL
¾ cup	all-purpose flour	175 mL
¼ cup	rice flour	50 mL
¼ cup	chopped macadamia nuts	50 mL
2 tsp	confectioner's (icing) sugar	10 mL

1. In a large bowl, cream butter and brown sugar until light and fluffy. Beat in egg and vanilla.

2. In a separate bowl, combine both flours and nuts. Stir into creamed mixture until well mixed. (Dough will be slightly sticky.)

3. Drop 8 mounds of dough in 1 tbsp (15 mL) measures onto lightly greased oven pan.

4. Bake on inverted bottom rack in preheated 350°F (180°C) toaster oven for 12 to 15 minutes, or until light golden. Turn pan halfway through baking time. Let cookies cool on pan for 5 minutes before transferring to a rack. When cool, dust with confectioner's sugar. Refrigerate or freeze remaining dough or continue to bake batches until all dough is used.

> **Storing Nuts**
>
> To keep nuts fresh, wrap in small freezer bags and store in the refrigerator or freezer for up to eight weeks.

Lemon Poppy Seed Cookies

Refrigerator cookies are ideal for the toaster oven, since you just need to cut a few slices and you'll have freshly baked cookies in a flash. Freeze or refrigerate the raw dough and bake the cookies as you need them. If you wish, dust with sifted confectioner's (icing) sugar before serving.

Cookies make great hostess gifts. Wrap them in small plastic bags and tie with a ribbon or raffia with a handmade tag. Pair cookies with tea, coffee, chocolate or a fancy mug.

**MAKES ABOUT
72 COOKIES**

1 cup	butter, softened	250 mL
⅓ cup	granulated sugar	75 mL
2 cups	sifted cake flour	500 mL
2 tbsp	poppy seeds	25 mL
1 tbsp	grated lemon zest	15 mL

1. In a large bowl, beat butter and granulated sugar until light and fluffy. Add flour, poppy seeds and lemon zest. Stir just until combined.

2. Divide dough into thirds. Place one piece on a large sheet of waxed paper. Using paper as a guide, form dough into a log 8 inches (20 cm) long. Repeat with remaining dough. Refrigerate logs for 3 hours or until firm.

3. Cut one log into slices ⅓ inch (8 mm) thick. Place 10 slices on lightly greased oven pan.

4. Bake on inverted bottom rack in preheated 350°F (180°C) toaster oven for 15 minutes, or until lightly browned. Turn oven pan halfway through baking time. Let cookies sit on pan for 5 minutes before transferring to a rack. Wrap and refrigerate remaining dough (or freeze for up to a month) or continue to bake cookies.

White Chocolate Pecan Blondies

This is a light-colored version of brownies. Chewy and buttery, they are practically candy. I like to serve them with fresh fruit.

MAKES 25 SQUARES

½ cup	butter, softened	125 mL
1 cup	packed brown sugar	250 mL
2	eggs	2
1 tsp	vanilla	5 mL
1¼ cups	all-purpose flour	300 mL
½ tsp	baking soda	2 mL
¼ tsp	salt	1 mL
¾ cup	chopped white chocolate (about 4 oz/125 g)	175 mL
½ cup	chopped pecans	125 mL
1 tbsp	confectioner's (icing) sugar	15 mL

1. In a large bowl, cream together butter and brown sugar until light and fluffy. Beat in eggs one at a time. Stir in vanilla.

2. In a separate bowl, combine flour, baking soda, salt, chopped chocolate and pecans. Stir into butter mixture just until combined. Spoon into a lightly greased and parchment-lined 8-inch (2 L) square baking pan.

3. Bake on inverted bottom rack in preheated 325°F (160°C) toaster oven for 35 minutes, or until a cake tester inserted in center comes out clean. Turn pan halfway through baking time. Cool in pan before cutting into squares. Sift confectioner's sugar over bars just before serving.

Parchment Paper

When you are baking bars or squares, line the baking pan with parchment paper so that the paper covers the bottom and two sides of the pan. Do not let the paper hang over the edges of the pan. After baking, run a knife around the inside of the pan and lift out the whole recipe in one big square. Place on a cutting board and cut into serving pieces. Trim off any crispy edges and eat as the cook's treat.

Lemon Bars

Usually the first to disappear from any sweet tray, lemon bars can also be cut into bite-sized squares. They cut best when cold.

These bars can be covered and refrigerated for up to three days or wrapped well and frozen for up to three weeks.

MAKES 25 BARS

Base

1 cup	all-purpose flour	250 mL
½ cup	confectioner's (icing) sugar	125 mL
½ cup	cold butter, cut in ½-inch (1 cm) pieces	125 mL

Filling

3	eggs	3
1 cup	granulated sugar	250 mL
2 tbsp	all-purpose flour	25 mL
1 tbsp	grated lemon zest	15 mL
⅓ cup	lemon juice	75 mL

1. To prepare base, in a food processor, pulse together flour and confectioner's sugar to combine. Add butter and process until butter is in tiny bits and pastry is just starting to come together.

2. Press pastry into bottom of a lightly greased and parchment-lined 8-inch (2 L) square baking pan.

3. Bake on inverted bottom rack in preheated 325°F (160°C) toaster oven for 30 minutes, or until lightly browned. (This will smell like shortbread.) Cool for 20 minutes so crust does not get soggy.

4. Meanwhile, for filling, in a medium bowl, whisk together eggs and granulated sugar until smooth. Gradually whisk in flour, lemon zest and juice.

5. Pour lemon mixture over baked base. Return to oven and continue to bake at 325°F (160°C) for 25 to 30 minutes, or until filling is lightly colored and set. Turn pan halfway through baking time. Cool on a rack.

6. Before cutting into bars, run a knife around edges and remove the whole recipe from pan. For a very clean cut, use a sharp knife that has been dipped in hot water.

Date Ginger Bars

These spice and fruit bars are reminiscent of hermit cookies. The softened dates help make them moist. The bars can be covered and refrigerated for up to three days or wrapped well and frozen for up to three weeks.

MAKES 25 BARS

¾ cup	chopped dates	175 mL
¼ cup	chopped candied ginger	50 mL
½ cup	boiling water	125 mL
1 cup	all-purpose flour	250 mL
1½ tsp	baking powder	7 mL
¾ tsp	ground cinnamon	4 mL
¼ tsp	ground nutmeg	1 mL
¼ tsp	ground allspice	1 mL
¼ tsp	salt	1 mL
⅓ cup	butter, softened	75 mL
½ cup	granulated sugar	125 mL
1	egg, beaten	1
½ tsp	vanilla	2 mL
Garnish		
2 tsp	confectioner's (icing) sugar	10 mL
½ tsp	ground cinnamon	2 mL

1. In a small bowl, combine dates, candied ginger and boiling water. Let stand for 10 minutes.
2. In a separate bowl, combine flour, baking powder, cinnamon, nutmeg, allspice and salt.
3. In a large bowl, beat together butter and granulated sugar until light. Stir in egg, vanilla and date mixture. Add dry ingredients and mix until just combined.
4. Spoon batter into a lightly greased and parchment-lined 8-inch (2 L) square baking dish.
5. Bake on inverted bottom rack in preheated 350°F (180°C) toaster oven for 25 minutes, or until a cake tester inserted in center comes out clean. Turn pan halfway through baking time. Cool in pan on rack.
6. In a small bowl, combine confectioner's sugar and cinnamon. Sift over cooled bars.

Rocky Road Bars

This is really a brownie that has been embellished with lots of goodies. The batter can be mixed right in the saucepan before being spooned into the baking dish.

Cover and refrigerate for up to two days or cut into bars, wrap tightly and freeze for up to three weeks.

MAKES 25 BARS

⅓ cup	butter	75 mL
5 oz	bittersweet or semisweet chocolate, coarsely chopped	150 g
¾ cup	granulated sugar	175 mL
1 tsp	vanilla	5 mL
½ cup	all-purpose flour	125 mL
Pinch	salt	Pinch
2	eggs, beaten	2
½ cup	chopped pecans	125 mL
½ cup	chocolate chips	125 mL
1 cup	mini marshmallows	250 mL
2 oz	semisweet chocolate, melted	60 g

1. In a large heavy saucepan, melt butter and chocolate together over medium heat. Remove from heat.

2. Stir in sugar, vanilla, flour, salt and eggs. Add pecans, chocolate chips and marshmallows. Stir just until combined. Spoon into a lightly greased and parchment-lined 8-inch (2 L) square baking dish.

3. Bake on inverted bottom rack in preheated 350°F (180°C) toaster oven for 25 to 30 minutes, or until a cake tester inserted in center comes out clean. Top may seem a bit soft, but do not overbake. Turn pan halfway through baking time. Cool in pan on rack.

4. When cool, drizzle melted chocolate over brownies in a zigzag pattern. Cool again before cutting into bars.

Butterscotch Coconut Bars

There was always fresh fruit and a sweet treat waiting for us when we came home from school. My mother used to make a version of this that we called candy cake, because the chewy, moist, cakelike bars were the closest thing we had to real candy.

Cover and refrigerate for up to one day, or wrap well and freeze for up to three weeks.

MAKES 25 BARS

½ cup	butter	125 mL
¾ cup	packed brown sugar	175 mL
2	eggs, beaten	2
1 tsp	vanilla	5 mL
¾ cup	all-purpose flour	175 mL
½ tsp	baking soda	2 mL
¼ tsp	salt	1 mL
1 cup	butterscotch chips or chocolate chips	250 mL
½ cup	unsweetened shredded coconut	125 mL

1. In a saucepan, melt butter over medium heat. Add brown sugar and cook for 2 to 3 minutes, or until mixture bubbles, stirring constantly. Remove from heat and cool in pan for 15 minutes.

2. Add eggs and vanilla, stirring to combine.

3. In a bowl, combine flour, baking soda and salt. Stir into egg mixture. Add chips and coconut and stir until combined.

4. Spoon mixture into a lightly greased and parchment-lined 8-inch (2 L) square baking dish.

5. Bake on inverted bottom rack in preheated 350°F (180°C) toaster oven for 30 minutes, or until a cake tester inserted in center comes out clean. Top should be soft, so do not overbake. Turn halfway through baking time. Cool in pan on rack before cutting into squares.

Desserts

Cinnamon Pecan Coffee Cake

Coffee cakes are multipurpose. They can be served as a dessert or as a "bread" at brunches and buffets. I have taken this to many a family reunion accompanied by a large bowl of fresh fruit cocktail and brought home the empty dishes. If nuts are a problem, simply omit them.

This cake can be covered and stored at room temperature for a day, or cut it into portions, wrap well and freeze. (The cake can also be frozen whole, but remove it from the pan before freezing.)

MAKES ONE 8-INCH (20 CM) SQUARE CAKE

½ cup	butter, softened	125 mL
¾ cup	granulated sugar	175 mL
2	eggs	2
1 tsp	vanilla	5 mL
1½ cups	all-purpose flour	375 mL
1½ tsp	baking powder	7 mL
1 tsp	baking soda	5 mL
¼ tsp	salt	1 mL
1 cup	sour cream or unflavored yogurt	250 mL
¼ cup	packed brown sugar	50 mL
2 tsp	ground cinnamon	10 mL
¼ cup	chopped pecans or walnuts	50 mL

1. In a large bowl, beat together butter and granulated sugar until light and fluffy. Beat in eggs one at a time. Beat in vanilla.

2. In a separate bowl, stir together flour, baking powder, baking soda and salt. Add to butter mixture alternately with sour cream, making three dry additions and two liquid additions. Mix just until combined.

3. In a separate small bowl, combine brown sugar, cinnamon and nuts.

4. Spoon half of batter into a lightly greased and parchment-lined 8-inch (2 L) square baking dish. Sprinkle half of nut mixture over batter. Spread remaining batter over top and sprinkle with remaining nuts.

5. Bake on inverted bottom rack in preheated 350°F (180°C) toaster oven for 45 minutes, or until a cake tester inserted in center comes out clean. Turn cake pan halfway through baking time. Cool in pan on rack.

Pineapple Upside-down Cake

Keep a can of pineapple chunks on hand to make this homey treat. For an old-fashioned look, sprinkle ⅓ cup (75 mL) halved maraschino cherries over the pineapple.

This cake is best served the day it is made.

MAKES ONE 9-INCH (23 CM) ROUND CAKE

⅓ cup	butter, melted	75 mL
¾ cup	packed brown sugar	175 mL
1	14-oz (398 mL) can pineapple chunks, drained	1
2 tsp	grated lemon zest, divided	10 mL
½ cup	butter, softened	125 mL
⅔ cup	granulated sugar	150 mL
2	eggs	2
1 tsp	vanilla	5 mL
1½ cups	all-purpose flour	375 mL
1½ tsp	baking powder	7 mL
½ tsp	baking soda	2 mL
¼ tsp	salt	1 mL
¾ cup	buttermilk or unflavored yogurt	175 mL

1. Pour melted butter into a deep 9-inch (1.5 L) round cake pan. Sprinkle with brown sugar, pineapple chunks and 1 tsp (5 mL) lemon zest.

2. In a large bowl, cream together butter and granulated sugar until light. Beat in eggs one at a time. Stir in vanilla and remaining 1 tsp (5 mL) lemon zest.

3. In a separate bowl, combine flour, baking powder, baking soda and salt. Add to creamed mixture alternately with buttermilk, making three dry additions and two wet. Mix after each addition just until combined.

4. Spread batter over pineapple.

5. Bake on inverted bottom rack in preheated 350°F (180°C) toaster oven for 35 minutes, or until a cake tester inserted in center comes out clean. Turn pan halfway through baking time. Let stand for 5 minutes before inverting onto a serving plate.

Pear Ginger Cake

Many people have a hard time imagining baking in something as small as a toaster oven. But if you have the all-purpose 8-inch (2 L) square baking pan, it is easy to make cakes like this one. The baked cake can be covered and kept at room temperature for a day or wrapped well and frozen whole or in pieces.

Serve this moist cake with applesauce, pear sauce or ice cream. It is delicious served warm or at room temperature.

MAKES ONE 8-INCH (20 CM) SQUARE CAKE

¼ cup	butter, melted	50 mL
½ cup	granulated sugar	125 mL
1	egg	1
⅓ cup	fancy molasses	75 mL
2 tbsp	finely chopped gingerroot	25 mL
1	ripe pear, unpeeled, finely chopped	1
¾ cup	milk	175 mL
1¾ cups	all-purpose flour	425 mL
1 tsp	baking soda	5 mL
1 tsp	ground cinnamon	5 mL
¼ tsp	salt	1 mL

1. In a large bowl, mix together melted butter and sugar until sugar is dissolved. Beat in egg. Stir in molasses, ginger, pear and milk. (Mixture may appear curdled.)

2. In a separate bowl, combine flour, baking soda, cinnamon and salt. Add to wet ingredients and mix until just combined.

3. Spoon batter into a lightly greased and parchment-lined 8-inch (2 L) square baking dish.

4. Bake on inverted bottom rack in preheated 375°F (190°C) toaster oven for about 40 minutes, or until a cake tester inserted in center comes out clean. Turn pan halfway through baking time. Cool in pan on rack.

Mediterranean Orange Cake

Breadcrumbs are the unusual ingredient in this moist orange cake. If possible, use bread that is a couple of days old.

This cake makes a perfect finale to a light meal. You can serve it with sliced fresh strawberries or slightly sweetened pureed frozen strawberries. Other fresh fruit such as blueberries, raspberries or sliced melon make colorful additions.

Store the baked cake, covered, in the refrigerator for up to three days, or wrap individual pieces, store in a container and freeze for up to a month. Defrost the pieces as needed for an instant treat.

MAKES ONE 8-INCH (20 CM) ROUND CAKE

4	eggs	4
¾ cup	vegetable oil	175 mL
2 tbsp	grated orange zest	25 mL
1½ cups	fresh breadcrumbs	375 mL
1 cup	confectioner's (icing) sugar	250 mL
¾ cup	ground almonds	175 mL
1½ tsp	baking powder	7 mL
½ tsp	ground cinnamon	2 mL
½ cup	orange juice	125 mL
¼ cup	granulated sugar	50 mL

1. In a large bowl, beat together eggs, oil and orange zest.

2. In a separate bowl, combine breadcrumbs, confectioner's sugar, almonds, baking powder and cinnamon. Add to egg mixture and stir until just mixed.

3. Pour batter into a lightly greased and parchment-lined deep 8-inch (20 cm) round cake pan.

4. Bake on inverted bottom rack in preheated 350°F (180°C) toaster oven for 30 to 35 minutes, or until a cake tester inserted in center comes out clean. Turn pan halfway through baking time. Cool cake in pan for 5 minutes. Run a knife around edge and turn onto a cake plate.

5. Meanwhile, combine orange juice and granulated sugar in a small saucepan. Bring to a boil over high heat and stir to dissolve sugar. Remove from heat and cool slightly.

6. Prick cake all over with a skewer. Spoon syrup over cake gradually, while cake is cooling.

One-bowl Chocolate Mocha Cake

Any recipe that requires just one bowl is a favorite of any cook and dishwasher. Dust this popular cake (sometimes known as wacky cake) with confectioner's sugar or, for a double chocolate hit, drizzle with chocolate sauce or spread with chocolate cream cheese icing.

This cake can be covered and kept at room temperature for up to a day or wrapped well and frozen for up to a month.

MAKES ONE 9-INCH (23 CM) ROUND CAKE

1½ cups	all-purpose flour	375 mL
¾ cup	granulated sugar	175 mL
⅓ cup	cocoa powder, sifted	75 mL
1 tbsp	instant coffee powder	15 mL
1 tsp	baking soda	5 mL
½ tsp	salt	2 mL
⅓ cup	vegetable oil	75 mL
1 tsp	white vinegar	5 mL
1 cup	cold water	250 mL

1. In a large bowl, combine all ingredients. Beat with an electric mixer on medium-high speed for 3 minutes, scraping bottom and sides of bowl occasionally.

2. Spoon batter into a greased and parchment-lined deep 9-inch (23 cm) round cake pan.

3. Bake on inverted bottom rack in preheated 375°F (190°C) toaster oven for 23 to 25 minutes, or until a cake tester inserted in center comes out clean. Cool in pan for 10 minutes. Loosen cake around outside edge with a knife and turn cake out onto a rack to cool completely.

Chocolate Cream Cheese Icing

In a large bowl, beat together 4 oz (125 g) softened cream cheese and 2 oz (60 g) melted semisweet chocolate. Beat in 1 tbsp (15 mL) strong coffee and 1 cup (250 mL) confectioner's (icing) sugar. Makes enough icing for one 9-inch (23 cm) round cake.

Blueberry Almond Crisp

Instead of using only blueberries, try a combination of fruits such as blueberries and peaches, blueberries and raspberries or raspberries and peaches. If you are using juicy fruits like peaches, stir in an extra tablespoon of flour. Serve with orange-flavored yogurt cheese.

If you are using frozen blueberries, do not defrost before using.

MAKES 6 SERVINGS

4 cups	fresh or frozen blueberries	1 L
1 tbsp	all-purpose flour	15 mL
2 tsp	lemon juice	10 mL
½ tsp	almond extract	2 mL
Topping		
1 cup	rolled oats (not instant)	250 mL
½ cup	packed brown sugar	125 mL
¼ cup	all-purpose flour	50 mL
¼ cup	sliced or slivered almonds	50 mL
¼ cup	butter, melted	50 mL

1. Spread blueberries over bottom of a lightly greased 8-inch (2 L) square baking dish. Sprinkle berries with flour, lemon juice and almond extract. Stir to distribute flour.

2. To prepare topping, in a bowl, combine rolled oats, brown sugar, flour and almonds. Stir in melted butter. Spread topping over fruit.

3. Bake in preheated 350°F (180°C) toaster oven for 30 minutes, or until top is golden and blueberries are bubbling.

Orange Yogurt Cheese

Place 1 cup (250 mL) unflavored yogurt in a sieve lined with cheesecloth, coffee filter or paper towel and place sieve over a bowl (or use a yogurt strainer). Cover and refrigerate for 3 to 4 hours. Place drained yogurt in a bowl. Stir in 1 tsp (5 mL) grated orange zest, 2 tbsp (25 mL) orange juice and 1 tbsp (15 mL) granulated sugar. Cover and refrigerate until using. Makes about ½ cup (125 mL).

Apple Ginger Crisp

Apples and ginger are a winning combination, and the gingersnap cookies add a sparkle and are a change from the usual rolled-oat topping. Ripe pears are a good substitute for apples.

Serve this hot, warm or at room temperature, plain or with vanilla ice cream or orange yogurt cheese (page 189).

MAKES 4 SERVINGS

5	medium apples, peeled and sliced (about 6 cups/1.5 L)	5
¼ cup	granulated sugar	50 mL
½ tsp	ground cinnamon	2 mL
1 cup	coarse gingersnap crumbs	250 mL
¼ cup	all-purpose flour	50 mL
¼ cup	butter, melted	50 mL

1. In a lightly greased 8-inch (2 L) square baking dish, combine apples, sugar and cinnamon.
2. In a bowl, combine gingersnap crumbs, flour and melted butter. Stir to combine. Sprinkle topping over apples. Cover tightly with foil.
3. Bake in preheated 375°F (190°C) toaster oven for 30 minutes. Remove foil and continue to bake for 15 minutes, or until apples are tender. Let stand for 10 minutes before serving.

Peach Melba Cobbler

French chef Auguste Escoffier used poached peaches and raspberry sauce to create the famous dessert for the Australian opera singer Nellie Melba. A stunning color combination, these two fruits are combined for the base of this cobbler.

Raspberries give off a lot of juice, so make the cobbler at least four hours before serving so the dessert can cool and set. If you are using frozen raspberries, use individually frozen berries rather than frozen berries packed in syrup.

MAKES 5 SERVINGS

4 cups	fresh or frozen (slightly defrosted) raspberries	1 L
2 cups	sliced peeled peaches or nectarines	500 mL
½ cup	granulated sugar	125 mL
3 tbsp	all-purpose flour	45 mL
Topping		
1 cup	all-purpose flour	250 mL
4 tbsp	granulated sugar, divided	60 mL
1 tsp	baking powder	5 mL
Pinch	salt	Pinch
¼ cup	butter, cold, cut in pieces	50 mL
½ cup	milk	125 mL
½ tsp	vanilla	2 mL

1. In a large bowl, toss together raspberries, peaches, sugar and flour. Spoon into a lightly greased 8-inch (2 L) square baking dish.

2. To prepare topping, in a separate bowl, combine flour, 3 tbsp (45 mL) sugar, baking powder and salt.

3. Add butter to flour mixture and cut in using a pastry blender or two knives until mixture is in tiny bits.

4. In a small bowl or measuring cup, combine milk and vanilla. Pour into dry ingredients and mix with a fork just until mixture comes together in a loose batter.

5. Drop batter by spoonfuls over fruit. Sprinkle with remaining 1 tbsp (15 mL) sugar.

6. Bake in preheated 375°F (190°C) toaster oven for about 35 minutes, or until fruit is bubbling at edges and topping is cooked (gently lift center of topping to make sure dough is cooked underneath).

Apple Crumble Pie

Use Northern Spy, Golden Delicious or Ida Reds in this wonderful apple pie.

MAKES ONE 9-INCH (23 CM) PIE

Make Ahead

Make and roll the pastry and make crumb topping a day ahead. Cover and refrigerate. On bake day, prepare apples, assemble and bake pie.

5	medium apples, peeled and sliced (about 6 cups/1.5 L)	5
¼ cup	granulated sugar	50 mL
2 tbsp	all-purpose flour	25 mL
½ tsp	ground cinnamon	2 mL
1	unbaked 9-inch (23 cm) pie shell, storebought or homemade	1

Topping

¾ cup	all-purpose flour	175 mL
⅓ cup	packed brown sugar	75 mL
¼ tsp	ground nutmeg	1 mL
⅓ cup	butter, cold, cut in pieces	75 mL

1. In a large bowl, combine apples, granulated sugar, flour and cinnamon. Spoon into pie shell, mounding slightly in center.

2. For crumble topping, in a separate bowl, combine flour, brown sugar and nutmeg. Using a pastry blender or two knives, cut in butter until mixture forms lumps the size of small peas. Sprinkle topping over apples.

3. Bake in preheated 400°F (200°C) toaster oven for 20 minutes. Reduce heat to 350°F (180°C) and continue to bake for about 50 minutes, or until topping is golden and apples are tender and bubbling. Serve warm or at room temperature.

All-purpose Pastry

In a large bowl, combine 1½ cups (375 mL) all-purpose flour and 1 tsp (5 mL) salt. Add ¼ cup (50 mL) cubed cold butter and ¼ cup (50 mL) cubed cold lard. Cut in fat using a pastry blender or two knives until mixture is in tiny bits.

In a small measuring cup, combine 1 tsp (5 mL) lemon juice or white vinegar and ⅓ cup (75 mL) ice water. Sprinkle over flour mixture and combine gently with a fork until mixture starts to come together. If mixture is too dry, add water 1 tsp/5 mL at a time until mixture can be formed into a ball.

On a lightly floured surface, roll pastry into a 12-inch (30 cm) circle. Line a 9-inch (23 cm) pie plate and double pastry over at rim to make a high fluted edge. Refrigerate pastry until using.

Pineapple Samurai

This is a version of a very popular dessert served at the hotel where I worked in Australia. It was served with prescooped servings of ice cream and garnished with washed and trimmed pineapple leaves. Since macadamia nuts were plentiful, a spoonful of coarsely chopped nuts was also sprinkled over each serving.

This dessert is a breeze to make, and you can just pop it into the toaster oven at the last minute. If you are using orange juice, remember to grate the zest before you juice the orange.

MAKES 2 TO 3 SERVINGS

Make Ahead

Pineapple version can be assembled up to 4 hours before baking.

Variation

Bananas Samurai
In place of the pineapple, use two slightly underripe bananas. Cut each banana in half lengthwise and then widthwise (you'll have 8 pieces in total). Bake for 8 to 10 minutes, or until bananas are hot and just starting to soften.

½	golden pineapple, peeled, cored and cut in 1-inch (2.5 cm) pieces	½
⅓ cup	packed brown sugar	75 mL
1 tsp	grated orange zest	5 mL
¼ cup	orange juice or mango juice	50 mL
2 tbsp	lime juice or lemon juice	25 mL
2 tbsp	butter, cut in pieces (optional)	25 mL
2 tbsp	toasted shredded coconut	25 mL
	Fresh mint leaves	

1. Arrange pineapple pieces in a lightly greased 8-inch (2 L) square baking dish. Sprinkle with brown sugar, orange zest, orange juice, lime juice and butter, if using.

2. Bake in preheated 425°C (220°C) toaster oven for 15 minutes, or until juices are bubbling.

3. Arrange on serving dishes and garnish with coconut and mint leaves.

Peaches with Amaretti Cookies

Peaches and almonds are a happy combination. Amaretti cookies are meringue cookies full of almond flavor (look for them in Italian food shops), and they make an easy crisp topping for baked fruit. Serve these peaches with ice cream, frozen yogurt, yogurt cheese (page 189) or citrus tea bread (page 163).

MAKES 4 SERVINGS

7	peaches, peeled and sliced	7
2 tbsp	lemon juice	25 mL
¼ cup	packed brown sugar, divided	50 mL
1 cup	amaretti cookie crumbs (about 18 cookies)	250 mL
2 tbsp	butter, melted	25 mL
¼ tsp	ground nutmeg or mace	1 mL

1. In a lightly greased shallow 6-cup (1.5 L) baking dish, combine sliced peaches, lemon juice and 2 tbsp (25 mL) brown sugar.

2. In a medium bowl, combine cookie crumbs, remaining 2 tbsp (25 mL) brown sugar, melted butter and nutmeg. Sprinkle over peaches.

3. Bake in preheated 400°F (200°C) toaster oven for 15 minutes, or until peaches are just cooked. Serve warm or at room temperature.

Peeling Peaches

To peel peaches, place in boiling water for 30 seconds. Plunge peaches into a bowl of ice water and cool. The skins should slip off easily.

Baked Apples

Sometimes a forgotten dessert, baked apples are an appealing addition to any dessert table. If the apples are browning too much, reduce the oven temperature to 325°F (160°C) toward the end of the baking time. Serve warm with ice cream or yogurt cheese (page 189).

MAKES 4 SERVINGS

4	apples (e.g., Northern Spy, Ida Red or Golden Delicious)	4
¼ cup	pure maple syrup	50 mL
¼ cup	apricot jam	50 mL
¼ cup	apple juice or water	50 mL
2 tbsp	lemon juice	25 mL
¼ tsp	ground nutmeg	1 mL

1. Core apples using a corer or melon ball scoop. Using a sharp knife, score peel about a third of the way down apples (this prevents apples from bursting). Arrange apples in a shallow baking pan that will hold juices.

2. In a small bowl, combine maple syrup, jam, apple juice, lemon juice and nutmeg. Spoon into center of apples, letting remainder drizzle over.

3. Bake in preheated 375°F (190°C) toaster oven for 30 minutes. Spoon glaze over apples. Bake for another 15 to 20 minutes, or until apples are tender. (Timing will depend on variety and size of apples.)

Pears with Honey and Rosemary

This is a good weeknight dessert, when you want a little treat but do not feel like baking. Use ripe pears and fresh rosemary if you can. Serve with crusty bread and cheese.

Make sure you grate the zest from the lemon before juicing the fruit.

MAKES 4 SERVINGS

4	ripe pears (Bartlett or Anjou)	4
¼ cup	lemon juice	50 mL
¼ cup	honey	50 mL
2 tbsp	water	25 mL
2 tsp	grated lemon zest	10 mL
1 tsp	chopped fresh rosemary, or ½ tsp (2 mL) dried	5 mL

1. Peel pears, cut in half and remove cores. Arrange pears cut side up in an 8-inch (2 L) square baking dish.

2. In a small bowl, combine lemon juice, honey and water. Drizzle honey mixture over pears. Sprinkle with lemon zest and rosemary. Cover tightly with foil.

3. Bake in preheated 375°F (190°C) toaster oven for 30 minutes, or until pears are just tender. (Timing depends on ripeness of pears.) Remove from oven and spoon juices over pears. Cool at room temperature or in refrigerator.

Pears

Plan ahead when cooking with pears, as they are often sold unripe. At home, store them in a brown paper bag with an apple, at room temperature, to encourage ripening. Check daily for ripeness. (The pear should give slightly when gently pressed.)

Vanilla Custard

A satisfying and soothing dessert. Top with fresh raspberries or blueberries.

MAKES 4 SERVINGS

2	eggs	2
2	egg yolks	2
1½ cups	milk or light (5%) cream	375 mL
¼ cup	granulated sugar	50 mL
1 tsp	vanilla	5 mL
Pinch	salt	Pinch
Pinch	ground nutmeg	Pinch

1. In a large bowl, beat together eggs, egg yolks, milk, sugar, vanilla, salt and nutmeg. Pour into four 4-oz (125 mL) ramekins.

2. Place ramekins in an 8-inch (2 L) square baking dish. Do not crowd dishes. Pour boiling water into baking dish until it comes halfway up sides of ramekins.

3. Bake in preheated 350°F (180°C) toaster oven for 35 minutes, or until custard is just set and knife inserted in center comes out clean.

4. Remove ramekins from water bath and cool on wire racks. Cover and refrigerate for 4 hours or until completely chilled.

Sticky Toffee Pudding

Not really a pudding, but a dense cake served with a toffee sauce. This is a version developed by my friend Bill Vronsky after chef training in Ireland, where the pudding was served in most pubs and restaurants. The beauty of it is that it can be cut into serving pieces and packaged in freezer containers, so there is always a dessert on hand.

This dessert is rich, so serve small portions. Use dark brown sugar (such as Demarara or Muscovado) if you have it.

MAKES 8 SERVINGS

Cake

¾ cup	chopped dates	175 mL
¾ cup	hot tea	175 mL
¾ tsp	baking soda	4 mL
1 tsp	vanilla	5 mL
1 tsp	ground or instant coffee powder	5 mL
⅓ cup	butter, softened	75 mL
¾ cup	packed brown sugar	175 mL
2	eggs	2
1 cup	all-purpose flour	250 mL
1 tsp	baking powder	5 mL
¼ tsp	salt	1 mL

Toffee Sauce

¼ cup	butter	50 mL
½ cup	packed brown sugar	125 mL
½ cup	corn syrup	125 mL
½ cup	whipping (35%) cream	125 mL
1 tsp	vanilla	5 mL

1. In a small bowl, combine dates and hot tea. Let stand for 10 minutes. Stir in baking soda, vanilla and coffee.
2. In a large bowl, cream together butter and brown sugar. Beat in eggs one at a time.
3. In a separate bowl, stir together flour, baking powder and salt.
4. Stir flour mixture into butter mixture and mix thoroughly. Add date mixture and combine well, scraping sides and bottom of bowl.

5. Spoon batter into a lightly greased and parchment-lined deep 8-inch (20 cm) round cake pan. Bake on inverted lower rack in preheated 375°F (190°C) toaster oven for 35 minutes, or until a cake tester inserted in center comes out clean. Turn pan halfway through baking time. Let stand in pan for 10 minutes before inverting onto a serving plate.

6. Meanwhile, to prepare sauce, in a small saucepan, melt butter on medium heat. Stir in brown sugar, corn syrup and whipping cream. Bring to a simmer and cook, stirring often, for about 6 minutes, or until sauce is smooth and velvety. Stir in vanilla.

7. Brush about $\frac{1}{3}$ cup (75 mL) sauce over top and sides of pudding. Serve with a spoonful of sauce. (This is best served at room temperature with warm sauce.)

Baked Alaska

Always a special dessert to serve for a birthday or celebration. Use your favorite ice cream or sherbet in the filling. Serve as is or with a chocolate or strawberry sauce or fresh berries.

Sponge cake cups are often found in the produce section, close to the berries; otherwise check the baking section.

MAKES 4 SERVINGS

Make Ahead

This dessert can be assembled and frozen for up to 8 hours or overnight.

4	sponge cake cups (about 3 inches/ 7.5 cm in diameter)	4
2 cups	ice cream or sherbet	500 mL
3	egg whites	3
¼ tsp	cream of tartar	1 mL
½ cup	granulated sugar	125 mL

1. Place cake cups on oven pan.
2. Using an ice-cream scoop, scoop ½ cup (125 mL) rounded measures of ice cream and arrange in center of cake cups. Place oven pan in freezer and freeze for 2 hours, or until firm.
3. In a large bowl, beat egg whites with cream of tartar until soft peaks form.
4. Gradually beat in sugar until stiff peaks form.
5. Spread egg whites over ice cream and cake, covering all surfaces. Return to freezer until baking time.
6. Bake in preheated 450°F (230°C) toaster oven for 4 to 5 minutes, or until just browned. Watch carefully and turn pan halfway through cooking time for even browning. Serve immediately.

Index

National Library of Canada Cataloguing in Publication

Stephen, Linda, 1945-
[125 best toaster oven recipes]
    150 best toaster oven recipes / Linda Stephen.

Includes index.
Previously published under title: 125 best toaster oven recipes.
ISBN 978-0-7788-0616-5 (softcover)

    1. Toaster oven cooking. 2. Cookbooks. I. Title. II. Title: One hundred fifty best
toaster oven recipes. III. Title: 125 best toaster oven recipes

TX840.T63S84 2018   641.5'86   C2018-901307-9